Introduction

I have been writing and presenting about Row-Level Security in Power BI for many years. Through the comments and feedback I got from my presentations and articles, I felt a need for a place to have everything gathered in one place. The lack of a book that explains everything about the current subject motivated me to end up gathering all my articles in this book. The result is what you are reading.

Row-Level Security in Power BI is not about sharing your content. It is, on the other hand, about sharing the same content with a different audience in the way that they see different views of the data. They will have different access to the data. Some of them might see the entire data, and some others might see part of the data that they are authorized to see.

Instead of creating multiple reports with the same format, fields, calculations, and visualizations, and only making them different in filtering, the correct way to do it is through row-level security. This will make sure you have the maximum consistency and minimum maintenance for your Power BI project.

This is not a book about theories. This is a hands-on book. There are tons of demos and examples with the code samples that you can try. You will learn through this book, what is row-level security. You will learn different types of security and patterns in which you will see the most common challenges for implementing the security and the solution to save them.

The book starts with the basics of row-level security, then you will learn about static vs. dynamic row-level security. You will learn patterns such as everyone see their own data, but the manager sees a different view or users and profiles for branch managers. Or the organizational hierarchy, or even the many-to-many relationship challenge of row-level security etc. through this book.

This book is not about how to create a report, build a visualization, connect to a dataset, or set up a gateway. If you want to learn those, I do recommend reading my other book: Power BI online book, from Rookie to Rock Star.

About the Author

Reza Rad is a Microsoft Regional Director, an Author, Trainer, Speaker and Consultant. He has a BSc in Computer engineering; he has more than 20 years' experience in data analysis, BI, databases, programming, and development, mostly on Microsoft technologies. He is a Microsoft Data Platform MVP for over nine continuous years (from 2011 till now) for his dedication to Microsoft BI. Reza is an active blogger and co-founder of RADACAD. Reza is also co-founder and co-organizer of the Difinity conference in New Zealand.

His articles on different aspects of technologies, especially on MS BI, can be found on his blog: https://radacad.com/blog.

He wrote some books on MS SQL BI and also is writing some others, He was also an active member on online technical forums such as MSDN and Experts-Exchange, and was a moderator of MSDN SQL Server forums, and is an MCP, MCSE, and MCITP of BI. He is the leader of the New Zealand Business Intelligence users group. He is also the author of very popular book Power BI from Rookie to Rock Star, which is free with more than 1700 pages of content and the Power BI Pro Architecture published by Apress.

He is an International Speaker in Microsoft Ignite, Microsoft Business Applications Summit, Data Insight Summit, PASS Summit, SQL Saturday, and user groups. And He is a Microsoft Certified Trainer.

Reza's passion is to help you find the best data solution; he is a Data enthusiast.

Table of Contents

Table of Contents

Row-level Security Configuration in Power BI Desktop

One aspect of sharing is the security of the data set. Enabling different roles and giving users access to different levels of data is called Row-level Security. This chapter explains the details of this security method and how to configure it in Power BI Desktop. Row-level Security enables you to apply security to roles and adds users to each role. An example of that is when you want people from one branch, city, department, or store to be able to only see their part of the data and not the whole data set. Power BI applies that through a row-level security configuration on the Power BI model itself. So regardless of what source you are importing your data from, you can apply row-level security on it.

What's Good About Row-level Security in Power BI Desktop?

Row-level security is about applying security on a data row-level. For example sales manager of united states, should only see data for the United States and not for Europe. The Sales Manager of Europe won't be able to see sales in Australia or the United States. And someone from the board of directors can see everything. The reason was that Row-level Security wasn't part of the Power BI model. Now in the new version of Power BI Desktop, the security configuration is part of the model and will be deployed with the model.

Prerequisite

For this example, I will use the AdventureWorksDW excel sample data source. You can download it from here.

Create a Sample Report

Let's start by creating a sample report in Power BI Desktop from the AdventureWorks Excel file. I only select DimSalesTerritory, and FactResellerSales for this example;

☐ ⊞ DimSalesReason

☑ ⊞ DimSalesTerritory

☐ ⊞ DimScenario

☐ ⊞ FactAdditionalInternationalProductDescription

☐ ⊞ FactCallCenter

☐ ⊞ FactCurrencyRate

☐ ⊞ FactFinance

☐ ⊞ FactInternetSales

☐ ⊞ FactInternetSalesReason

☐ ⊞ FactProductInventory

☑ ⊞ FactResellerSales

☐ ⊞ FactSalesQuota

without any changes in Power Query editor, let's load it in the report, and build a simple column chart with Sales Amount (from FactResellerSales), and Country (from DimSalesTerritory).

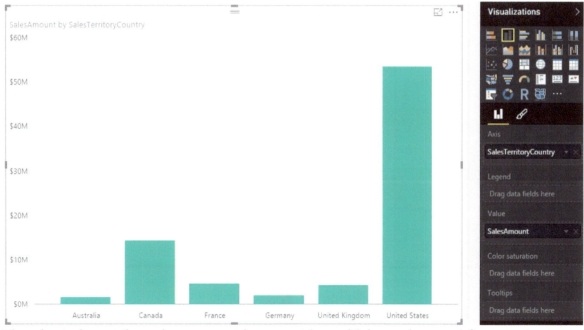

The chart shows the sales amount by countries, which can be used for creating row-level security on Geo-location information easily. Now let's add one card visualization for total Sales Amount. And two slicers (one for Sales Territory Group, and the other one for Sales Territory Region). Below screenshot is the layout of this sample report now;

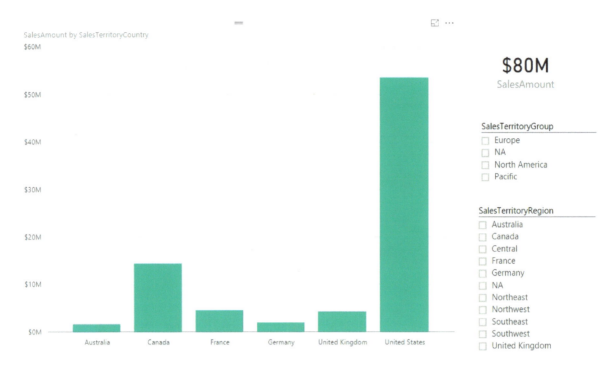

Our total Reseller sales amount in this view is $80M, and we have sales values for Australia, Canada, France, Germany, the UK, and the USA. Now let's create roles.

Creating Roles

Now let's create roles for that. Our goal here is to build roles for the sales manager of the USA and Europe. They should each only see their group or country in the data set. For creating roles go to the Modeling tab in Power BI Desktop. You will see a section named Security there;

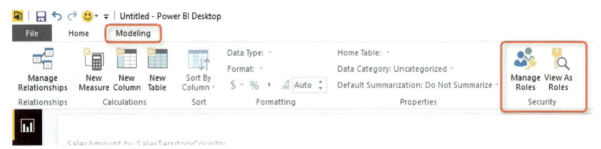

Click on Manage Roles to create a new role. You will see Manage Roles window which has three panes as below

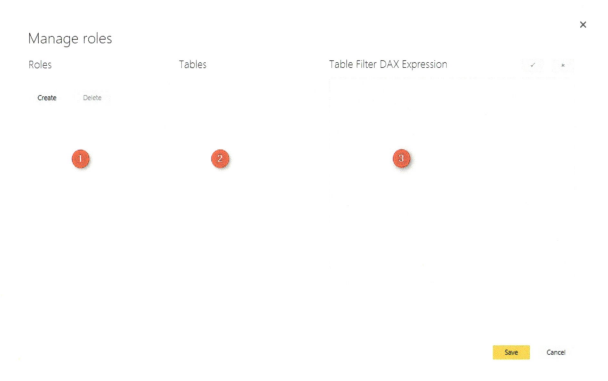

You can create or delete roles in numbered one pane, You can see tables in your model (marked with number two) (for this example you will see two tables only, but not now, after creating the first role), and then you can write your DAX filtering expression (marked with number three). Yes, you have to write DAX code to filter data for each role, but this can be very simple DAX expressions.

Now Create a Role, and name it as "USA Sales Manager", you will see two tables in the Tables section: FactResellerSales, and DimSalesTerritory. With a click on the ellipsis button on each table, you can create DAX filters for each column. From DimSalesTerritory, create a filter for Country.

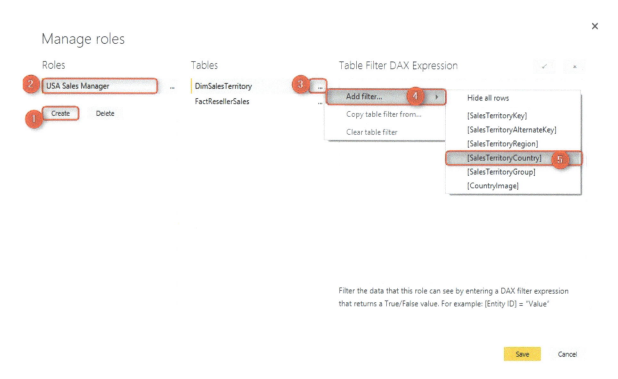

Now in the DAX Filter expression, you will see an expression created automatically as [SalesTerritoryCountry] = "Value", change the value to the United States, and apply.

Now create another role, name it as Europe Sales Manager, put a filter on SelesTerritoryGroup this time, and change Value to "Europe" as below;

Testing Roles in Desktop

Great, we have created our two sample roles. Now let's test them here. Yes, we can test them in Power BI Desktop with View As Roles menu option. This option allows us to view the report exactly as the user with this role will see. We can even combine multiple roles with seeing a consolidated view of a person who has multiple roles. Go to the Modeling tab, and choose View As Role option.

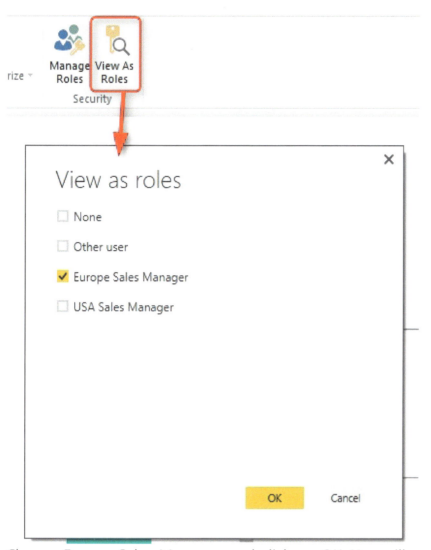

Choose Europe Sales Manager, and click on OK. You will see sales for Europe only showing with a total of $11M, and showing only countries Germany, UK, and France.

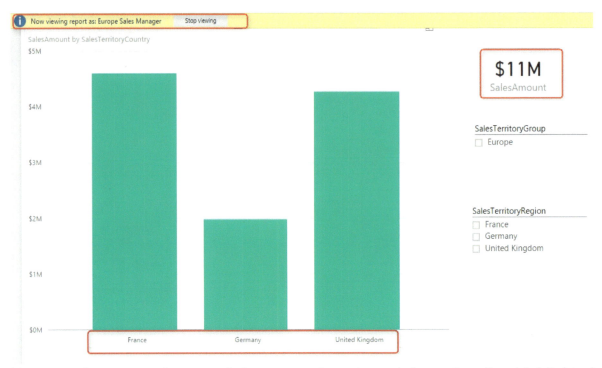

You can also see at the top of the report there is an information line highlighted showing that the view is Europe Sales Manager. If you click stop viewing, you will see the report as a normal view (total view).

Power BI Service Configuration

Roles should be assigned to Power BI users (or accounts in other words), and this part should be done in Power BI Service. Save and publish the report into Power BI. I named this report as RLS PBI Desktop. You can name it whatever you want. After publishing the report, click on Security for the data set.

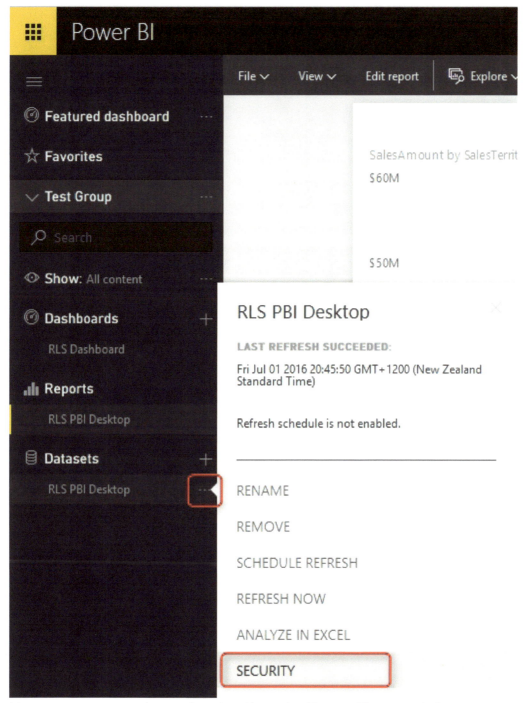

Here you can see roles and assign them to Power BI accounts in your organization.

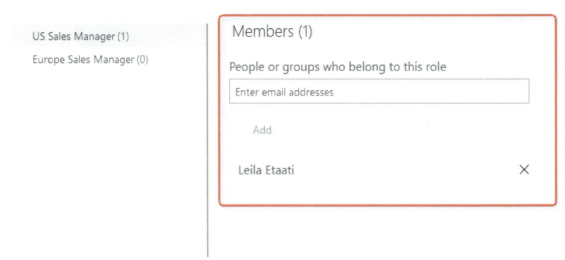

You can set each user to more than one role, and the user then will have a consolidated view of both roles. For example, a user with both roles for the USA and Europe sales manager will see data from All Europe and the USA.

Test Roles in Power BI Service

You can also test each role here, just click on the ellipsis button beside each role, and click on Test as Role.

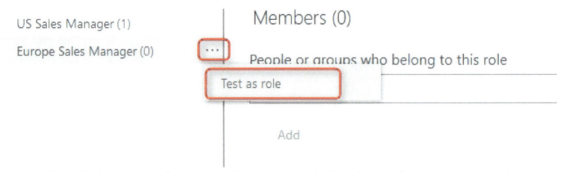

Test As Role will show you the report in view mode for that role. As you see, the blue bar shows that the report showed the role of Europe Sales Manager. You can change it there if you like.

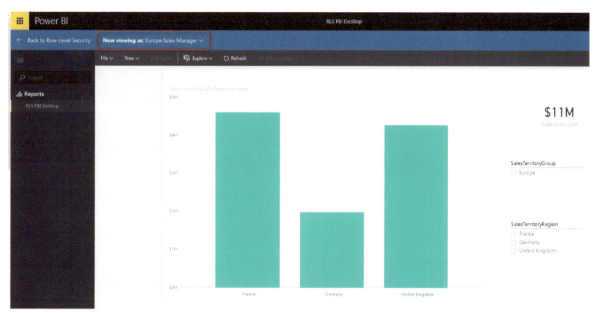

With setting users for each role, now your role level security is ready to work. If the user login with their account, they will only see data for their roles.

Re-Publish Won't Hurt

As I mentioned in the very first paragraph of this chapter, the great thing about this new feature is that RLS is part of the Power BI model. And if you publish your Power BI model again and again with changes, you won't lose configuration on the web. You also won't lose users assigned to each role, as long as you keep role names unchanged.

Summary

Row-level Security is giving users different views of the data from the same Power BI content. As you have learned in this chapter, implementing row-level security is simple. The reason this method is called Row-level security is because of the DAX filter applied to the data row-level.

In this chapter, you've learned about a specific type of row-level security called Static row-level security. It is called static, because the filter values are statically determined in DAX expressions. If you want to apply such filter for thousands of roles, then maintenance costs is very high. In ideal world, you want to be able to apply security based on the login of users automatically. In the next chapter, you will learn about Dynamic Row-level Security, which is the next step to apply security in more complex scenarios.

Dynamic Row-level Security with Power BI Made Simple

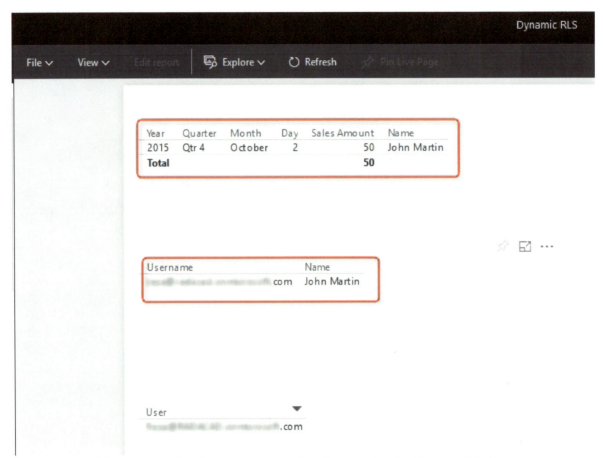

There are different methods to use row-level security in Power BI; You can set up multiple roles in the Power BI Desktop itself. However, row-level security defined in that way mentioned in the previous chapter isn't dynamic. By dynamic row-level security, I mean the definition of security be beside the user account information in the data source. For example, when John logs in to the system, based on data tables that show John is a sales manager for the specific branch, he should be able to see only those branch's data. This method is possible in Power BI using DAX UserName() or UserPrincipalName() function. In this chapter, I'll show you an example of dynamic row-level security with DAX USERNAME() function in Power BI.

Why Dynamic Row-level Security?

The most important question is why dynamic row-level security? To answer this question, you need to think about the limitation of static row-level security. The static row-level security is simple to implement; however, if you have thousands of roles, then it would be a nightmare to maintain. For example, if you want to create a payroll Power BI report, in a company with ten thousand users, you want every user to have his/her role. Dynamic row-level security is the answer to such scenarios.

Sample Data

For this example, I will use a data entered in Power BI itself. There won't be any external data sources. This doesn't mean that dynamic security has an issue with external data sources. Dynamic security works with any data sources as long as we have related data rows in the tables. However, if I use on-premises data sources, then half of this example should be explaining installation and configuration gateways, or if I use Azure data sources, then again, I have to explain how to set up that example. So just for the simplicity of this example, I'll be using data source inside Power BI.

For this example, let's create two simple tables; Sales Rep, and Transactions. Sales Rep has information from sales representatives, and transaction data is sales transactions. Obviously, each sales transaction handled by a sales rep. So let's create sample tables in Power BI. Open Power BI Desktop and from External Data section choose Enter Data.

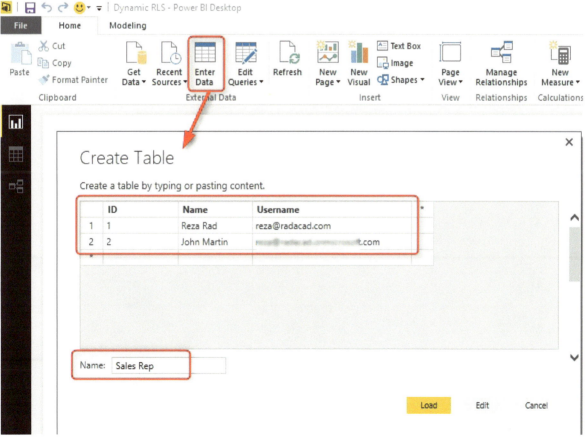

Create a table as above with three columns and data in it. You have to use usernames similar to Power BI accounts that you want to set up security for it. Name this table as Sales Rep.

Create another table for Transactions with the structure below, and name it Transactions:

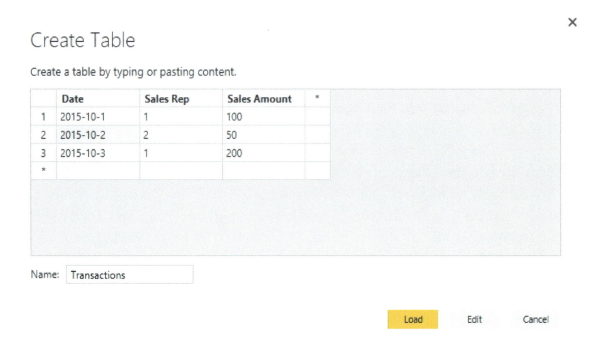

As you can see in the above screenshot, each sales transaction is handled by a sales rep. Again I mention that these tables are added inside Power BI just for simplicity of this example. Tables can come from everywhere.

Load tables into Power BI, we don't need to do anything with Power Query at this stage. Go to Relationship tab and verify the relationship between Sales Rep (ID) and Transactions (Sales Rep) to be as below;

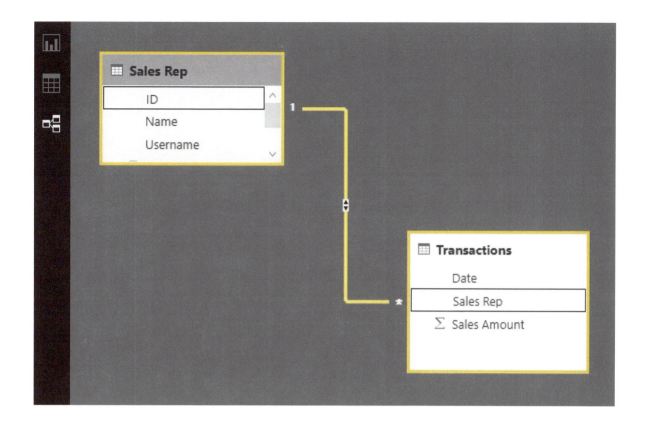

Sample Report

For this example, I will be using basic table visualization. The table visualization will show Date, Sales Amount (from Transactions), and Name (from Sales Rep). I also added another table visualization under that to show username, and Name (both from Sales Rep);

The main reason for this visualization is to simply show that each user will see only their data rows from all tables. I also will add a measure for USERNAME() in DAX to see the user logged in from my report. So in Data Tab, create a new measure, and name it User, with a value of USERNAME();

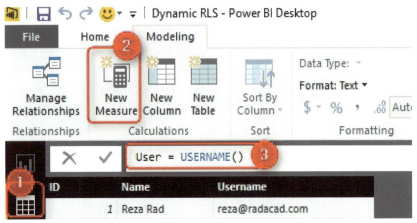

I also like to add date/time of refreshing the report with DAX NOW() function (note that NOW() function will return the server's current time, not the local. if you are interested in learning how to fetch local's current time, read here). So let's create new measure and name it Now;

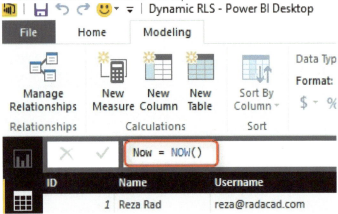

Now let's add two other table visualizations to the report. One for User, and another for Now. Here is the report's final view;

Year	Quarter	Month	Day	Sales Amount	Name
2015	Qtr 4	October	1	100	Reza Rad
2015	Qtr 4	October	2	50	John Martin
2015	Qtr 4	October	3	200	Reza Rad
Total				**350**	

Username	Name
reza@radacad.com	Reza Rad
~~████~~.com	John Martin

User
REZA-VAIO\Reza — Logged In User

Now
7/4/2016 10:42:33 PM — Refresh Date/Time

DAX Functions: UserName() and UserPrincipalName()

USERNAME() function in DAX returns the username of logged in user. However, there is a small trick for it. If we don't set up row-level security for our report, the USERNAME() function will return user id, which would be a unique identifier. To have an understanding of what I mean, publish your report to Power BI and browse it to see what you will see.

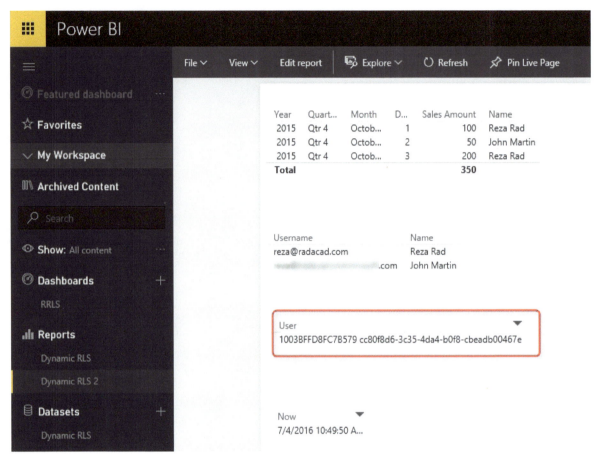

Without a security configuration on your report, you will see a unique identifier for the username, which isn't useful. Now let's set up row-level security and assign users to it to see how it works.

UserPrincipalName() function in DAX works exactly like UserName() function with the difference that it will always return the username (not the unique identifier). So basically, UserPrincipalName() is a better function for testing, but the works both the same in a production environment. Now let's set up row-level security and assign users to it to see how it works.

Row-level security in Power BI Desktop

I have explained in the previous chapter how row-level security in Power BI Desktop works. Here I will only use that technique to filter each role based on their username with DAX username() function. To create security, go to the Modeling tab (you need Power BI at least June 2016 update for this example), Manage Roles. Create a role and name it Sales Rep. and define a filter on Sales Rep table as below;

[Username] = USERNAME()

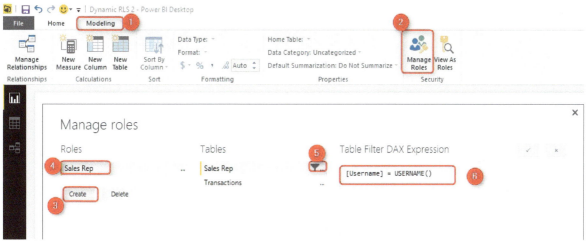

This filter simply means that the logged in user will only see his/her records in the whole data set. As you remember, the username field in Sales Rep table defined as usernames of Power BI accounts. And transactions table is also related to this table based on Sales Rep ID. So filtering one table will affect others. As a result, this single line filter will enable dynamic row-level security in the whole Power BI solution here.

Assign users to Power BI Security

Now Save, and publish your solution to Power BI. In Power BI service, go to the security setting of the data set you just published (I named this as Dynamic RLS).

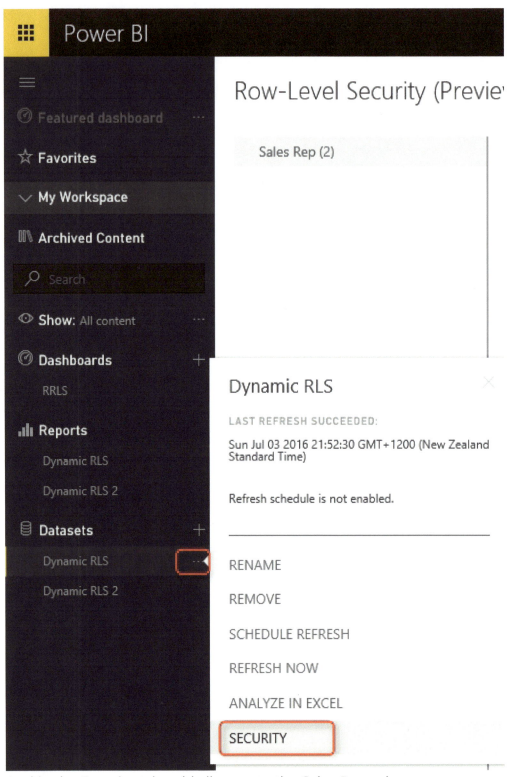

And in the Security tab, add all users to the Sales Rep role.

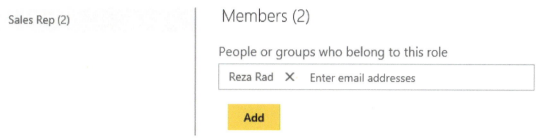

Note that adding a user here doesn't mean that they will see data in the report. Remember that this security is dynamic, means that they will see their data rows ONLY if the underlying data set has a record for their username, and they will only see data rows related to their username, not others.

Now, if you refresh the report in Power BI, you will see actual usernames. Because we already set up security for it, so it doesn't show unique identifiers anymore.

Share the Dashboard

Other users should have access to the dashboard and report first to see it. Create a dashboard from the main table in the report, name the dashboard as RLS (or whatever you would like to call it);

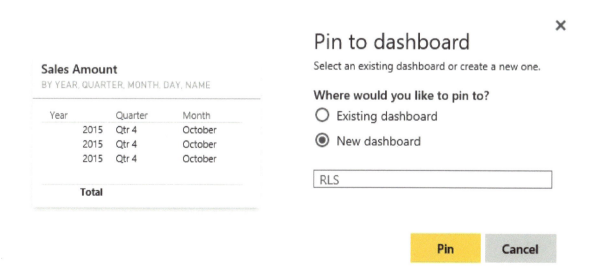

Now share the dashboard with other users

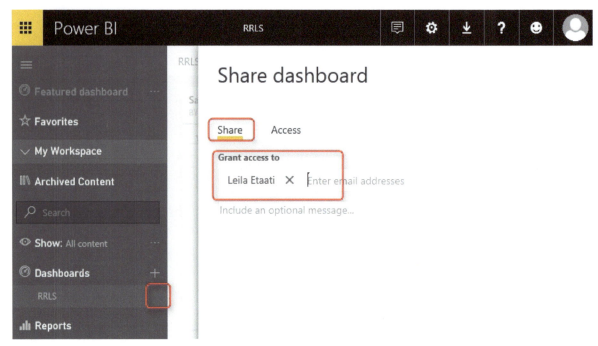

Test the Security

Now if other users open the report, and if their usernames match one of the entries in the Sales Rep table, they would see their names, and data rows related to that in the report;

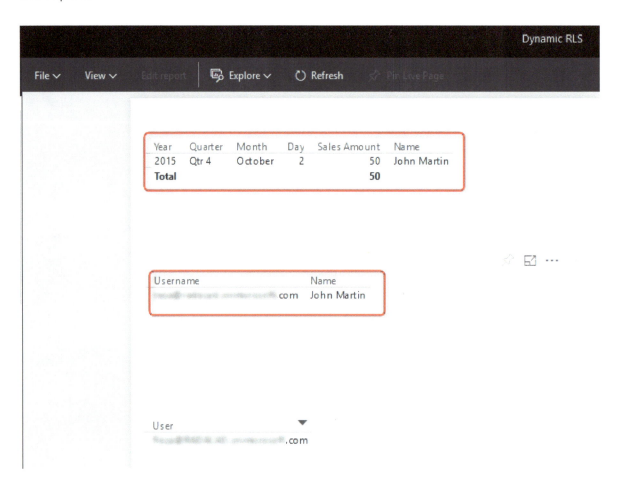

As you can see, John Martin only sees the transaction that he handled and his record in the Sales Rep table. The screenshot showed above is John's view of the Power BI report. While my view of this report would be different, I will see my two transactions and my name under Sales Rep.

Summary

You have seen how easy is to use Dynamic row-level security in Power BI using DAX USERNAME() or UserPrincipalName() function. With this method, users will see their view of the world. However, you need to make sure that your Power BI model has a relationship set up properly. Otherwise, people might see other table's data when there is no relationship between their profile table to those tables. Dynamic row-level security is highly dependent on your data model, so keep your data model right.

Dynamic Row-level Security with Manager Level Access in Power BI

Dynamic row-level security is not always that simple. This chapter is the next step from the previous chapter. I've had a lot of inquiries that; "What If I want users to see their own data, and the Manager to see everything?" or "How to add Manager or Director Level access to the dynamic row-level security?" This chapter will answer this question. In this chapter, you will learn a scenario that you can implement a dynamic row-level security. In this scenario, everyone will see their own data, but the manager will see everything.

Sample Dataset

To create a scenario with manager level access, and employee level access, I created two tables as below;

Sales Rep Table. This table has a field which is "Is Manager", values are zero or one. If the value is one, then the sales rep is a manager and can see everything if the value is zero, then the sales rep should be able to see his/her only data rows.

ID	Name	Email	Is Manager
1	Reza Rad	reza@radacad.com	0
2	Leila Etaati	leila@radacad.com	0
3	David	student1@radacad.com	0
4	Mark	student2@radacad.com	1

We also have a sales transaction table, which includes all transactions. there is a field in this table, which is the link to Sales Rep.

28

Date	Sales Rep	Sales Amount
1/01/2017	1	100
1/02/2017	2	300
1/03/2017	1	50

Relationship of these two tables are based on Sales Rep and ID field obviously

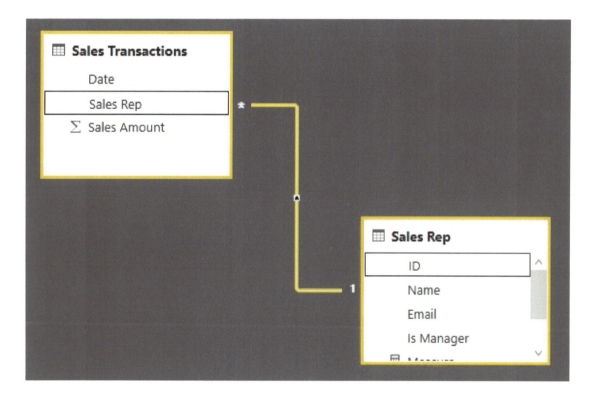

Creating the Role

As you can see in the data table, we can easily identify which sales transactions belongs to which sales rep. So a role logic to get only rows for every sales rep can be easily implemented with a DAX filter like this:

'Sales Rep'[Email]=Username()

I have explained that method previously in detail in the previous chapters. However, that method does not work when I have a "manager" level access too. For a manager level access, we can make some modifications. There are multiple ways of implementing it. This is one way of doing that;

The First Step; Identify the User

The very first step is always identifying who is the person logged into the report in Power BI Service. This can be done with *Username()* or *UserPrincipalName()* functions in DAX.

The Secon Step; Is the Logged In User, Manager, or Not?

We can use a DAX expression to identify is the person logged in, a manager, or not. This can be done with a simple MAXX expression as below;

MaxX(

Filter(

'Sales Rep',

'Sales Rep'[Email]=Username()

)

,'Sales Rep'[Is Manager]

)

In the expression above, we are using *FILTER()* to identify all rows from the sales rep table, where the email address matches the logged-in user. Then we get the maximum [Is Manager] value from that using *MAXX()* function. if the result of the expression above is 1, then the person is a manager, otherwise not.

If the User is not Manager, show only records related to the user

If the user is not a manager, then we just show the data related to him/her. this can be an expression as below;

'Sales Rep'[Email]=Username()

If the user is a manager, then show everything

an easy way of showing everything is writing a DAX expression that always returns true as a result. as simple as this;

1=1

All in One

Now if we combine all these codes and logic together, we end up with an expression as below;

If(

MaxX(

Filter(

'Sales Rep',

'Sales Rep'[Email]=Username())

,'Sales Rep'[Is Manager])=0,

'Sales Rep'[Email]=Username(),

1=1

)

The expression above will show everything to the manager and will only show related data to non-manager users.

You can create a role in Power BI under Sales Rep table with the expression above;

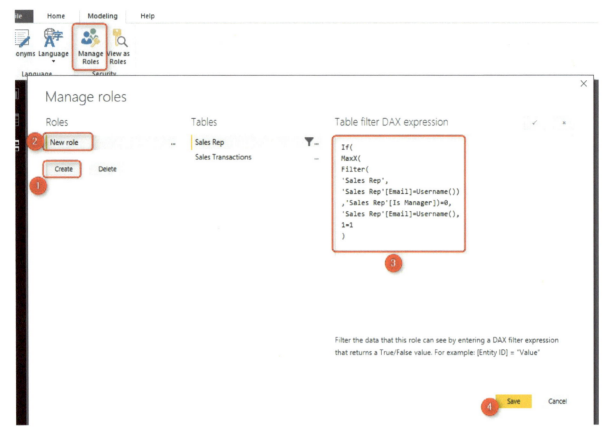

Test the Result

After creating this role, publish the report into Power BI, Go to Security configuration of the dataset;

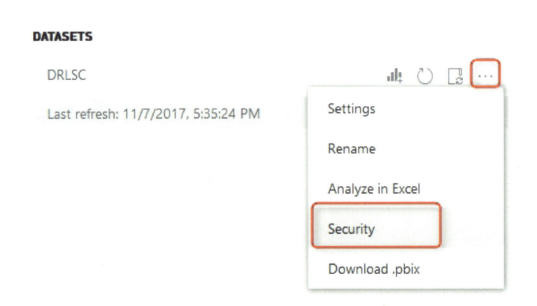

Add all users to the role. There will be no problem with doing this action. If the user is not in your Sales Rep list, they will not see anything. If they are, they will have restricted access.

Row-Level Security

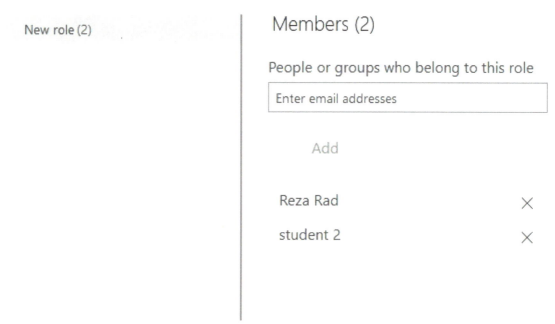

New role (2)

Members (2)

People or groups who belong to this role

Enter email addresses

Add

Reza Rad   ✕

student 2   ✕

Then share the dashboard also to all users.

This is what Reza (Restricted user who is not a manager) will see;

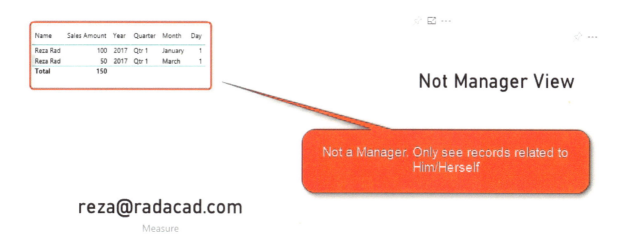

Name	Sales Amount	Year	Quarter	Month	Day
Reza Rad	100	2017	Qtr 1	January	1
Reza Rad	50	2017	Qtr 1	March	1
Total	**150**				

Not Manager View

Not a Manager. Only see records related to Him/Herself

reza@radacad.com

Measure

And this is what Mark (Manager user) will see;

Manager View

Manager will see all records from all users

student2@radacad.com
Measure

Summary

In summary, this was one of the patterns of the row-level security implemented dynamically. In this chapter, you've learned how you can implement a dynamic row-level security with a manager level access. This method implemented very simply, there are other ways of implementing it as well. In the next chapters, I'll write about other scenarios of RLS with multiple user profiles as well. If your Row-level Security requirement is different.

Dynamic Row-level Security with Profiles and Users in Power BI: Many-to-Many Relationship

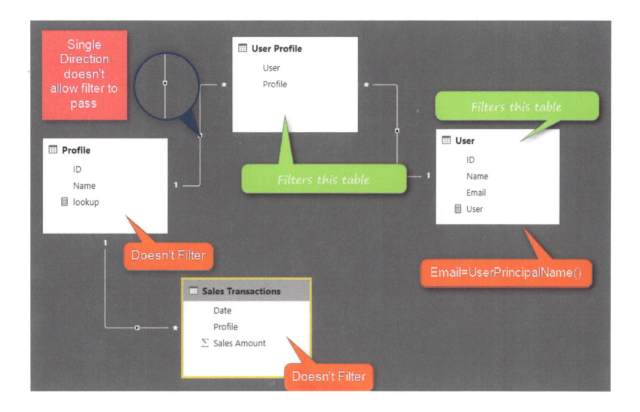

In this chapter, we are going to look at another type of security which deals with users and their profiles. Sometimes you have a user part of multiple groups (or profile), and also, a profile contains multiple users. This Many-to-Many relationship needs to be also incorporated in the way that security works in Power BI. You want all users to see data related to their own profiles. Because this model includes a Many-to-Many relationship, the implementation of that is a bit different from the normal Dynamic RLS.

Prerequisite

For reading this chapter, it would be much better to have an understanding of the simple dynamic row-level security with Username or UserPrincipalName function beforehand. Please read the chapter about dynamic row-level security.

Scenario

Imagine Mark is working in a company. Mark is part of the Sales Group in Seattle. He should see all sales transactions related to Seattle. Also, he is part of the sales group in Portland and should see the details of the transactions of Portland too. On the other hand side; there are other people which their access is different. David is part of the sales group of Chicago, and also Seattle. This situation creates a Many-to-Many relationship between user table and profile table such as below;

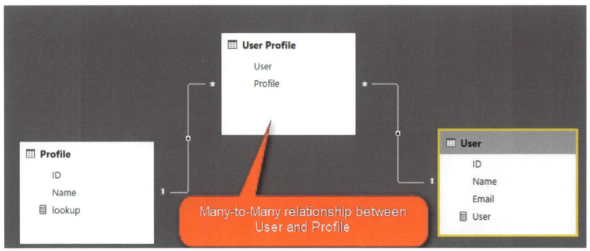

To be able to follow the example, here is sample data sets for each table;

User table

ID	Name	Email
1	Reza Rad	reza@radacad.com
2	Leila Etaati	leila@radacad.com
3	David	student1@radacad.com
4	Mark	student2@radacad.com

It is important that the user table includes a column for their Power BI accounts (in this example; email).

Profile table

ID	Name
1	Seattle Sales Manager
2	Chicago Sales Manager
3	Portland Sales Manager

You might call it a branch or store or group, as well.

User Profile table

User	Profile
1	1
4	1
2	2
3	2
1	3

This table holds the relationship or link between users and their profiles.

Transactions table

Date	Profile	Sales Amount
1/01/2017	1	100
1/02/2017	2	300
1/03/2017	1	50
1/04/2017	3	150

Every transaction is related to a profile. All users under that profile should have access to the transaction, which marked for that profile.

Full Diagram of the Model

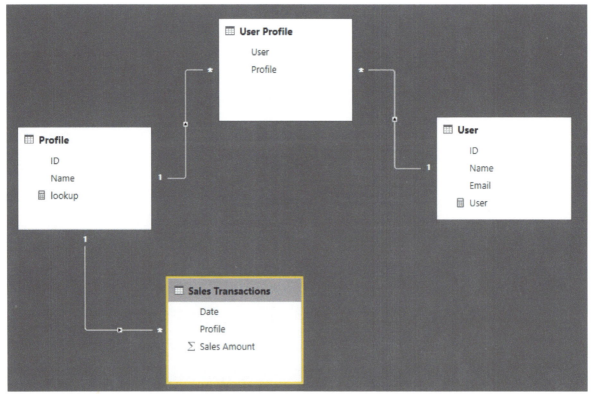

The difference between this model and a simple dynamic row-level security is that in this model, we have a Many-to-Many relationship, and filter propagation would not be as easy as the simple model.

Filtering Users doesn't work

Filtering users won't be a solution in this case. Here is a role defined in a user table with DAX filter below;

[email]=UserPrincipalName()

This DAX filter on the User table would filter the User Profile, but it won't filter the Profile table, so as a result, it won't filter the transaction table.

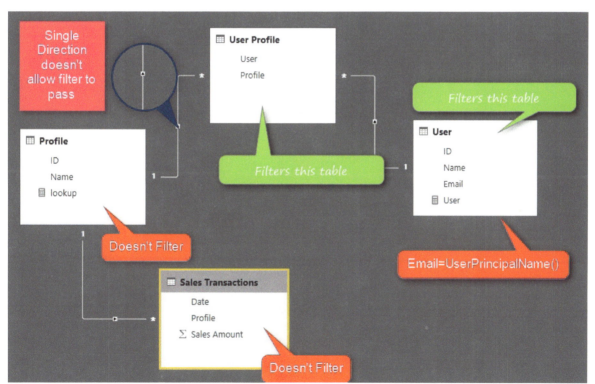

The direction of the relationship between the Profile table and User Profile table doesn't allow the filter to propagate from the User Profile to the Profile table. As a result, the Sales transactions table's data won't be filtered with the DAX filter defined in the user table. There are many methods that you can get this solution working. In this chapter, I'll explain two methods;

Cross Filter; or Both Direction Relationship

This method is not recommended, especially because of the performance issue. However, I like to explain it as the first method, because it helps to understand how relationships work in DAX. For using this method, you need to change the direction of the relationship between Profile table, and User Profile table to both directional, and also you need to check the option for "apply security filter in both directions".

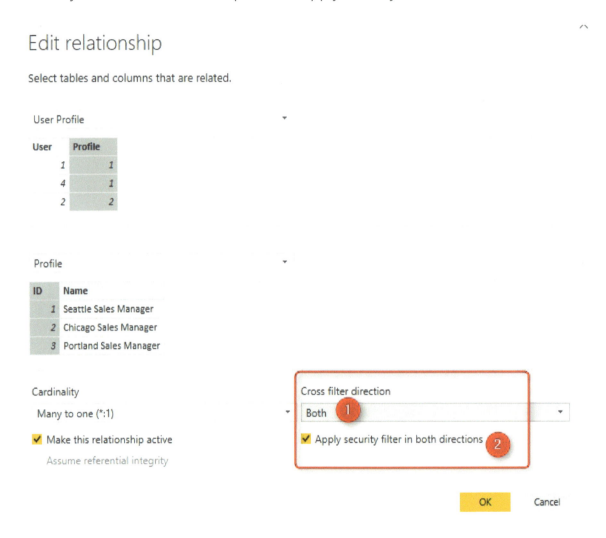

After this change your row-level security configuration will work perfectly fine as below;

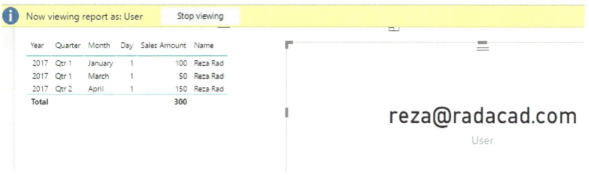

The diagram of the model is now passing the filter all the way to sales transactions table;

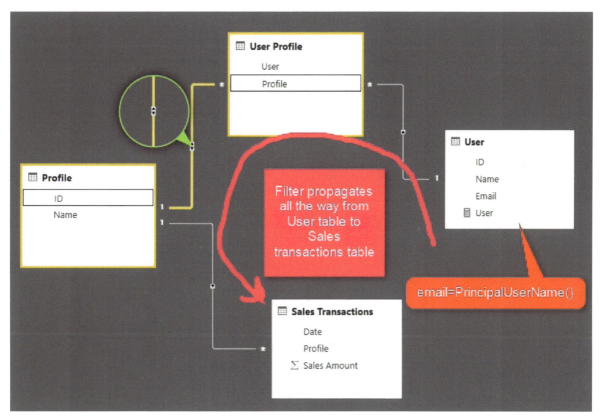

This method is easy to implement. However, is not recommended. Applying both direction relationship and the security filter will slow down the performance of your Power BI solution significantly. On the other hand side; if you have many tables related to each other, depends on the circular dependency, you might not be able to apply both directional relationships always. So I do recommend the next method.

Filtering Data through DAX

Because of the issues mentioned in the previous method, I do recommend using this method. This method is basically passing filters by writing some logic within DAX.

Dynamic Row-level Security with Profiles and Users in Power BI: Many-to-Many Relationship

There are many methods of implementing this logic with DAX. You can write a LookupValue function, Filter function, or many other ways. I'll explain it with the Filter function.

In this method, you don't need to change the direction of the relationship to be both directions. In this method, you need to find a way to filter data in the Profile table. If you filter the data in the Profile table, then the data in the Sales Transactions table will be filtered automatically. One way of filtering is to find out first all profile IDs from the User Profile which is related to the logged-in user;

Step 1: Find all rows in User Profile for the logged-in user

You can use a simple *FILTER()* function to get all rows from User Profile for the logged-in user;

FILTER(

>   *'User Profile',*

>   *RELATED(User[Email])=USERPRINCIPALNAME()*

)

This code will return a sub table from the User Profile table, which are only rows that is related to the logged-in user. from this list, let's get only their Profile ID in the next step;

Step 2: Get Profile IDs from the List

You can use *SelectColumns()* DAX function to only select Profile column (which is the ID of the profile);

SELECTCOLUMNS(

>   *FILTER(*

>   *'User Profile',*

>   *RELATED(User[Email])=USERPRINCIPALNAME()*

),

"Profile"

,[Profile]

)

Now this DAX code will return a table with a single column which is the ID of the profiles.

Step 3: Filter Profile table where the ID matches the table above

we can now use *IN* keyword to filter data of Profile table just for the logged-in user;

[ID] IN SELECTCOLUMNS(

      FILTER(

      'User Profile',

      RELATED(User[Email])=USERPRINCIPALNAME()

),

      "Profile"

,[Profile]

)

This filter should be written in the **Profile** table as below;

As a result, this method works perfectly as expected;

The diagram of this method is a single directional relationship. However, the DAX
Filter propagates all the way with the logic we've written in the role.

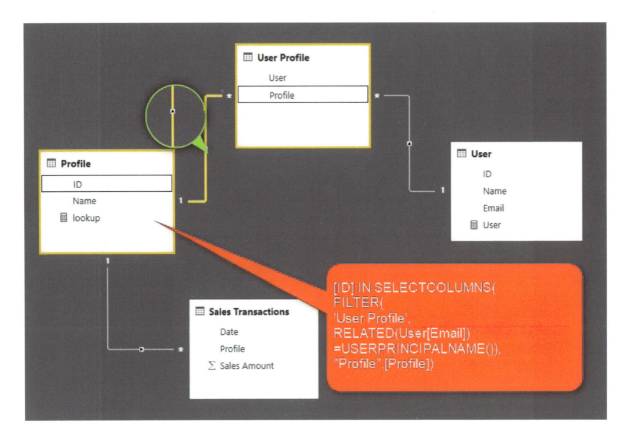

Summary

Applying row-level security has many variations. In this chapter, you've learned about
how to use Users and Groups (or Profiles) concept and overcome the Many-to-Many
challenge for the row-level security. You've learned about two methods, which one of
them was the recommended approach. There are other ways to implement this
scenario as well (with LookupValue and many other functions).

Dynamic Row-level Security with Organizational Hierarchy Power BI

In previous chapters, I covered some methods of Dynamic Row-level Security including Row-level Security user-based, With Manager Level Access, and also with User and Profiles as a many to many relationships. In this chapter, I'm going to cover another common scenario for row-level security; Organizational hierarchy for security. Through organizational hierarchy, the approach is that each employee should have access to his/her own data, and the manager should have access to employee's data; there might be another higher level manager as well. every person should have access to all employees under him or her. In this chapter, we are going to cover this method of security in detail with Power BI.

Prerequisite

For reading this chapter, it would be much better to have an understanding of the simple dynamic row-level security with Username or UserPrincipalName function beforehand. Please read the chapter about dynamic row-level security.

Scenario

Every company has an organizational hierarchy. In many scenarios employees needs to be authorized to their data records only and to the data of people whom they are managing. Here is an example of an organization chart;

In the organization chart above, Bill should see only one record of data. Mark should see three records; 2 records for himself and 1 record from Bill (because Bill is reporting directly to Mark). Leila should see 4 records; one record for herself, 2 records for Mark, and one record for Bill. This is how the hierarchical organizational row-level security required to work.

User Table

Here is the sample data in the User table;

ID	Name	Email	Manager ID
1	Reza Rad	reza@radacad.com	null
2	Leila Etaati	leila@radacad.com	null
3	David	student1@radacad.com	1
4	Mark	student2@radacad.com	2
5	Amy	student3@radacad.com	1
6	Bill	student4@radacad.com	4
7	Justin	student5@radacad.com	2
8	Lindsay	student6@radacad.com	5

as you can see, we have two main columns; ID of the employee and the Manager ID which points to the record which is the manager's record.

Sales Transaction Table

For every employee there might be one or more sales transactions in the transactions table;

Date	User	Sales Amount
1/01/2017	5	100
1/02/2017	6	300
1/03/2017	7	50
1/04/2017	8	150
2/04/2017	4	30
3/04/2017	3	340
4/04/2017	2	35
5/04/2017	1	20
10/04/2017	4	40

Diagram of the model

two tables here create a very simple diagram as below;

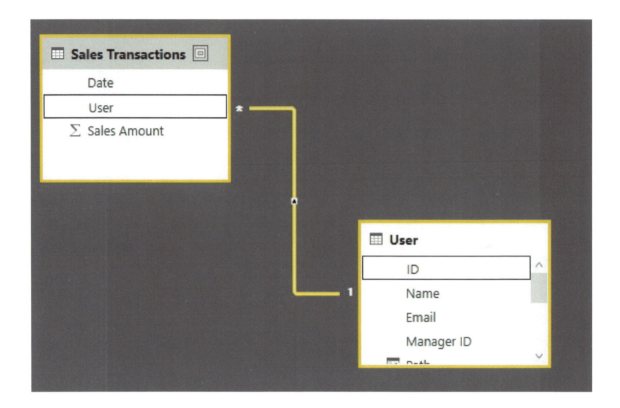

Sample Report

Here is a glance of the sample report; it has all records from all employees as well as the organizational hierarchy;

Name	Year	Quarter	Month	Day	Sales Amount
Amy	2017	Qtr 1	January	1	100
Bill	2017	Qtr 1	February	1	300
David	2017	Qtr 2	April	3	340
Justin	2017	Qtr 1	March	1	50
Leila Etaati	2017	Qtr 2	April	4	35
Lindsay	2017	Qtr 2	April	1	150
Mark	2017	Qtr 2	April	2	30
Mark	2017	Qtr 2	April	10	40
Reza Rad	2017	Qtr 2	April	5	20
Total					**1065**

Organization Chart

- ▲ ☐ Leila Etaati
  - ▲ ☐ Justin
    - ▲ ☐ Mark
      - ☐ Bill
- ▲ ☐ Reza Rad
  - ▲ ☐ Amy
    - ☐ Lindsay
  - ▲ ☐ David

Path Functions in DAX

For implementing row-level security in this scenario, one of the most common ways is using Path functions in DAX. Path functions are powerful functions that can navigate through an unknown level of hierarchy based on an ID and Parent ID structure. the structure of your data table usually is constructed based on two columns; ID and Manager ID as below;

ID	Name	Email	Manager ID
1	Reza Rad	reza@radacad.com	null
2	Leila Etaati	leila@radacad.com	null
3	David	student1@radacad.com	1
4	Mark	student2@radacad.com	2
5	Amy	student3@radacad.com	1
6	Bill	student4@radacad.com	4
7	Justin	student5@radacad.com	2
8	Lindsay	student6@radacad.com	5

To learn how path functions are working, let's explore a couple of these functions;

Path()

This function will go through an ID and parent ID structure and reveals the whole hierarchical path into a string type delimited style. to use this function, you can simply create a calculated column in the user table with below expression;

Path = PATH(User[ID],User[Manager ID])

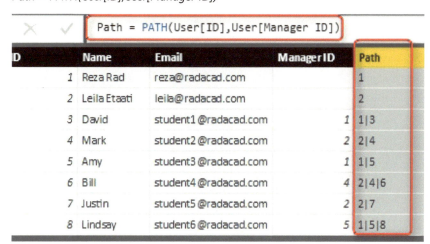

```
Path = PATH(User[ID],User[Manager ID])
```

D	Name	Email	Manager ID	Path
1	Reza Rad	reza@radacad.com		1
2	Leila Etaati	leila@radacad.com		2
3	David	student1@radacad.com	1	1|3
4	Mark	student2@radacad.com	2	2|4
5	Amy	student3@radacad.com	1	1|5
6	Bill	student4@radacad.com	4	2|4|6
7	Justin	student5@radacad.com	2	2|7
8	Lindsay	student6@radacad.com	5	1|5|8

This function will give you the whole path for the hierarchy with a delimited text value. The id of every employee in the path is separated in this text by a vertical line (|).

PathItem()

The *PathItem()* function will give you the specific item in a path. if you want to see who is the manager level 1 or level 2 or 3, you can use PathItem to fetch it. Here is an example;

PATHITEM(User[Path],2,1)

In the code above, 2 is the index of the level (2 means the second level of management), and 1 is the data type of output (1 means integer).

You can then combine this method with LookupValue function to find out the name of the person in that level;

LOOKUPVALUE(

User[Name],

User[ID],

PATHITEM(User[Path],2,1)

)

This means you can create calculated columns for every level of organization hierarchy;

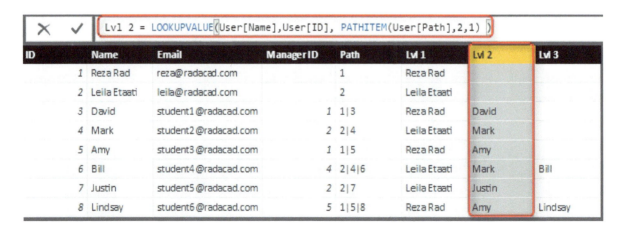

PathContains()

Now the important function of this chapter is PathContains. *PathContains* will check if an ID exists in the path or not. This is the function that you need to implement row-level security. All you need to find out is the ID of the person who is logged in. We already know how to get the email address of the person who is logged in, we use *UserName()* or *UserPrincipalName()* function for it.

Find out the ID of person Logged in

You can use a *Filter* function and Iterator function in DAX to find out who logged in to the system, filter function for filtering the user with the *PrincipalUserName()* function, and Iterator function fetched the ID of that remaining record.

Here is how Filter Function used to fetch the logged in user's record;

Filter(

User,

[Email]=USERPRINCIPALNAME()

)

After finding the record for the current user, you can use MaxX or MinX to find out the ID of that user;

MaxX(

Filter(

User,

[Email]=USERPRINCIPALNAME()

)

,User[ID]

)

and finally, you can now use this ID in a PathContains function to check if the user's ID exists in a path or not;

PATHCONTAINS(User[Path],

MaxX(

Filter(

User,

[Email]=USERPRINCIPALNAME()

)

,User[ID]

)

)

You need to add this logic as a role in User table;

This DAX expression will check the full path of the organization hierarchy to see if there are any records in the user table which has this user ID in their Path column or not.

Testing Result

As a result, if you switch to that user, you will see only logged in user with records related to him/her

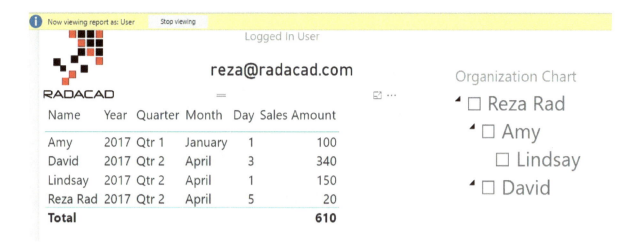

There are other methods of implementing such logic, and you can use other functions and expressions to find the current records ID. This chapter explained one way of doing this. As you can see in the above screenshot, Reza only has access to see records for himself, Amy, and David (his direct reports), and Lindsay (who reports directly to Amy).

Summary

Applying row-level security has many variations. In this chapter, you've learned about how to use organization hierarchy and Path functions in DAX to implement row-level security based on a hierarchy.

Dynamic Row-level Security in Power BI with Organizational Hierarchy and Multiple Positions in Many-to-Many Relationship – Part 1

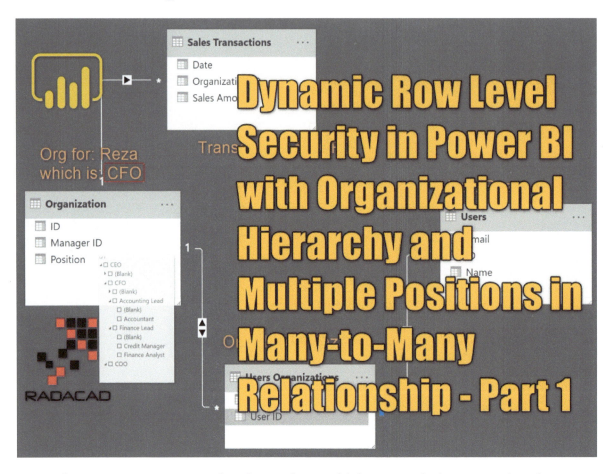

Recently I came across a couple of questions, which persuaded me to write about another pattern of dynamic RLS; When we have multiple positions for some users in the company, and each position is part of an organization hierarchy. When the user logins, we want him/her to see information about all his/her positions, and also the tree of positions under his/her organizational hierarchy. Don't think about this situation as a rare one. You already know some people in your company who take more than one role and have more than one manager then. So let's see how is it possible.

Prerequisite

The sample dataset for this example can be downloaded from here.

Scenario Explanation

Every organization has a hierarchy of employees based on their roles. Here is an example of such hierarchy:

Organization Chart

◢ ☐ Leila Etaati
    ☐ Justin
◢ ☐ Mark
    ☐ Bill
◢ ☐ Reza Rad
◢ ☐ Amy
    ☐ Lindsay
    ☐ David

However, the hierarchy is not always that simple. Sometimes (we can even say in most of the organizations) there are some people who have multiple roles. sometimes because they have been filling another role in the meantime while a replacement comes through. So the situation then will be like this, we will have a **User** table like below:

1²3 ID	ᴬᴮC Name	ᴬᴮC Email
2	Reza Rad	reza@radacad.com
1	Leila Etaati	leila@radacad.com
3	Jack Horlock	jack@radacad.com

We also have a table for positions and an organizational hierarchy as below; **Organization** Table;

1²3 ID	A^B_C Position	1²3 Manager ID
1	CEO	null
2	CFO	1
3	COO	1
4	Finance Lead	2
5	Accounting Lead	2
6	Accountant	5
7	Finance Analyst	4
8	Credit Manager	4

The Manager ID column in each row is a link to the ID field of another record in the same table representing the organizational hierarchy. the hierarchy of organization looks like below in action:

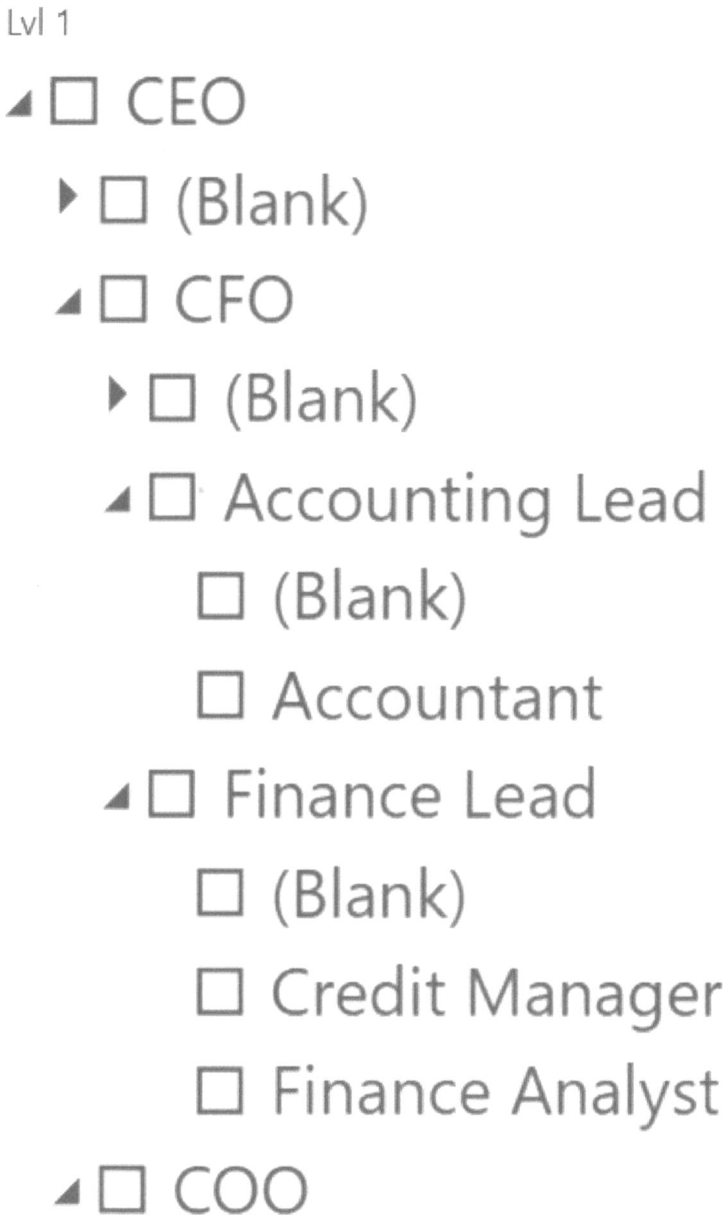

Lvl 1

▲ ☐ CEO

   ▶ ☐ (Blank)

  ▲ ☐ CFO

     ▶ ☐ (Blank)

    ▲ ☐ Accounting Lead

       ☐ (Blank)

       ☐ Accountant

    ▲ ☐ Finance Lead

       ☐ (Blank)

       ☐ Credit Manager

       ☐ Finance Analyst

  ▲ ☐ COO

Our transactions are related to the organization table. Let's assume we have sales records related to each role; **Sales Transaction** Table;

Date	Organization ID	Sales Amount
1/01/2017	5	100
1/02/2017	6	300
1/03/2017	7	50
1/04/2017	8	150
2/04/2017	4	30
3/04/2017	3	340
4/04/2017	2	35
5/04/2017	1	20
10/04/2017	4	40

As you can see, the transactions are related to Organization IDs not to the users specifically, because each user might be part of two organizations (multiple positions), or one organization (position) might have multiple users assigned to it.

The last table is the table that creates the many-to-many relationship between users and organizations (positions), User Organization table;

User ID	Organization ID
1	1
1	3
2	2
3	5
3	6

Here is the data model with the relationships;

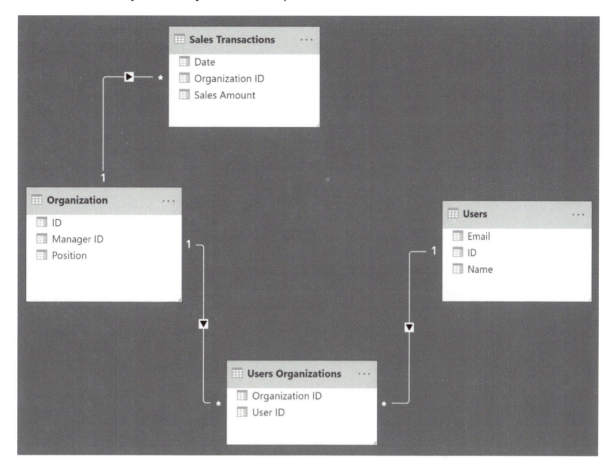

Sample

If, for example, in this dataset, Reza Logins, his user ID is 2, which is related to the organization role CFO, and should not see only transactions related to CFO, but also to other roles underneath it (Finance Lead, Accounting Lead, and etc.).

If Jack logins he has two organizational positions (Accounting Lead, and Accountant), and should see transactions related to both roles and also everything else in the hierarchy underneath these roles.

The Challenge

Dynamic Row-level Security means we get the username logged in using a function such as UserPrincipalName() or UserName() in DAX, and then filter tables based on that. If you like to learn about the basics of Dynamic RLS, read previous chapters about it. Now that you know the scenario above let's talk about what is the challenge we are facing in this implementation for security.

If we implement Dynamic RLS filtering in the user table, when a user such as Reza logins, then that table will be filtered and have only Reza's record in it. As a result, the User Organization table will be also filtered and will have only organizations that Reza is part of it. However, because of the single-directional relationship between the

User Organization table and the Organization table, the filter won't pass through the rest of the model. As a result, this user will see all organizations and all transactions regardless of RLS implemented in the user table! the diagram below shows this situation.

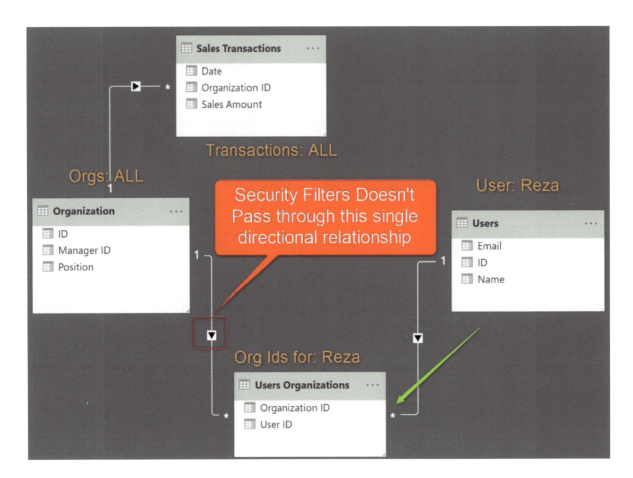

The many-to-many relationship in a model will bring the need for the both-directional relationship, which is not recommended.

If we change the relationship to both-directional then, we get another issue; Reza logins, he is associated with CFO organization, so will see the CFO only (because the both-directional relationship passes the filter), and will see only transactions of CFO. This is not what we want for this requirement.

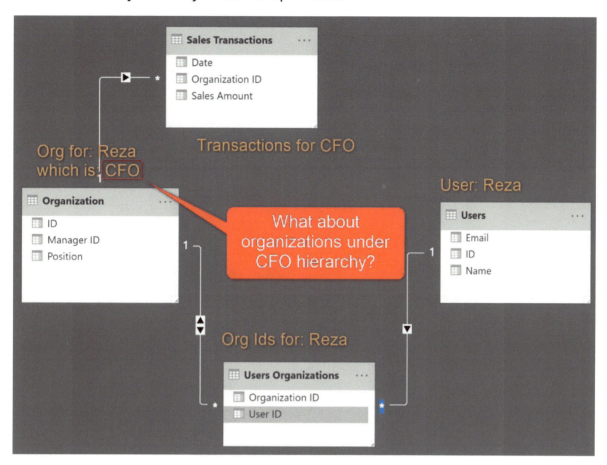

Reza should be able to see transactions of Finance Lead and Accounting Lead and other roles underneath. The both-directional relationship to the Organization table will filter the Organization table only for the current user's positions.

The both-directional relationship and organizational hierarchy don't work well with each other, as we need to see the entire tree of organization underneath.

The Solution

The both-directional relationship is not the solution, so I change the model to the single-directional as below;

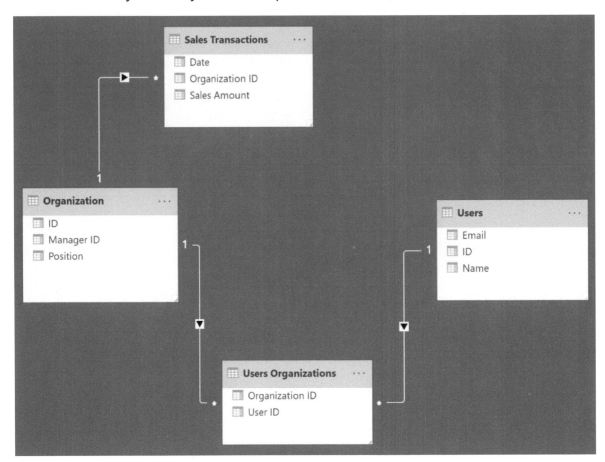

Now that you know the challenge and problem let's see how to fix it. The realm of dynamic row-level security is the realm of DAX. There is nothing to stop you from achieving what you want there. Your ability is only limited to your DAX skills. This problem can be solved using DAX too. However, the expression will be a bit long. To make it easier to understand, I break it into parts and will go through it step by step;

The realm of dynamic row-level security is the realm of DAX. There is nothing to stop you from achieving what you want there. Your ability is only limited to your DAX skills.

Step 1: Fetch the logged-in user's email address

Let's start with fetching the username; the measure below shows the logged-in username; Using the **UserPrincipalName()** DAX function;

Measure = USERPRINCIPALNAME()

```
1 Measure = USERPRINCIPALNAME()
```

reza@radacad.com

Measure

Step 2: Fetch the ID of the current user

Now as the second step, we need to find out what is the ID in the User table for the person logged in, which is achievable using **LookupValue()** DAX function;

Measure =

LOOKUPVALUE(

   Users[ID],

   Users[Email],

   USERPRINCIPALNAME()

)

LookupValue function has three parameters, the column that we want to fetch the value of it as output (ID), the column that we are searching for a value in it (Email), and the value itself (coming from UserPrincipalName() function). As a result, this shows the ID of the user logged in to the system;

```
1 Measure =
2 LOOKUPVALUE(
3     Users[ID],
4     Users[Email],
5     USERPRINCIPALNAME()
6 )
```

Returns the ID of the logged in user from the User table

Step 3: Fetch all Organization IDs which is associated with the current user

As the third step, we need to fetch all organization IDs (from the User Organization) table, which are associated with the current user. That means filtering the User Organization table where the User ID field matches the output of the previous step. We can achieve that using **Filter()** function in DAX;

Measure =

FILTER(

    'Users Organizations',

    'Users Organizations'[User ID]=

      LOOKUPVALUE(

        Users[ID],

        Users[Email],

        USERPRINCIPALNAME()

)

)

Filter function gets the table as the input (User Organization), and then the filter criteria, which would be the User ID, equals the output of the previous step calculation.

```
 1 Measure =
 2 FILTER(
 3          'Users Organizations',
 4          'Users Organizations'[User ID]=
 5              LOOKUPVALUE(
 6                  Users[ID],
 7                  Users[Email],
 8                  USERPRINCIPALNAME()
 9              )
10      )
```

Fetch All rows in the User Organization table which are associated with the current user

⚠ The expression refers to multiple columns. Multiple columns cannot be converted to a scalar value.

This gives us all rows in the User Organization table in which their User ID is equal to the ID of the current user. However, because the output of the Filter function, is a table, you cannot show it in a measure, that is why we get the error above. In this step, we are still in the middle of our way towards the final calculation. However, if you like to see what is the output of this so far, you can use the method below;

ConcatenateX a method to see some of the values in the table

This step is not part of the whole expression. It is just to show you how we can fetch the list of Organization IDs from the current table output of the Filter function using ConcatenateX (you can skip this step,)

Measure =

CONCATENATEX(

  FILTER(

    'Users Organizations',

    'Users Organizations'[User ID]=

      LOOKUPVALUE(

        Users[ID],

        Users[Email],

        USERPRINCIPALNAME()

)

    ),

    'Users Organizations'[Organization ID],

    ",")

ConcatenateX gets the table as input (the output of the previous step), then the expression that we want to concatenate it (the Organization ID column), and the text that we want to add between every two expressions to concatenate ("," as a comma separator).

```
 1  Measure =
 2  CONCATENATEX(
 3      FILTER(
 4              'Users Organizations',
 5              'Users Organizations'[User ID]=
 6                  LOOKUPVALUE(
 7                      Users[ID],
 8                      Users[Email],
 9                      USERPRINCIPALNAME()
10                  )
11          ),
12          'Users Organizations'[Organization ID],
13          ",")
```

ConcatenateX is a method to see the values in a column of the output table; in this case; Organization IDs that are in this list

As an example, if we have Leila logged in;

Her user ID is 1, and she has two Organization rows associated with her account, which will be the output of our calculation above;

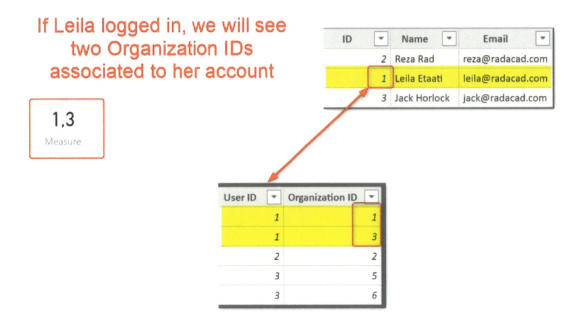

Next Steps

To avoid this chapter to become a very long one and hard to read the rest of this comes as the next chapter.

Dynamic Row-level Security in Power BI with Organizational Hierarchy and Multiple Positions in Many-to-Many Relationship – Part 2

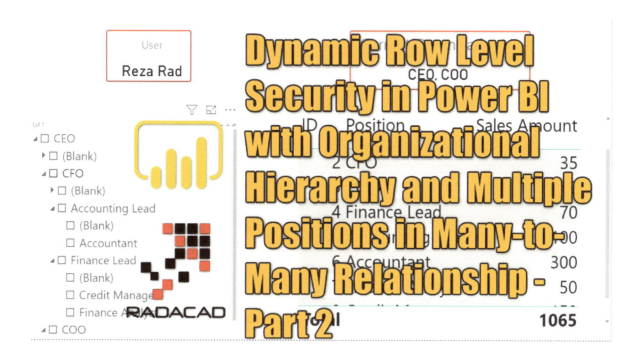

In the previous chapter, you learned about the challenge of security when Implementing it using multiple positions scenario combined with organizational hierarchy. We started to implement the solution using DAX in row-level security. This chapter is the second part of the solution.

Prerequisite

The sample dataset for this example can be downloaded from here. And read the previous chapter before starting this chapter.

Continuing the Solution

Expanding the Hierarchy

We need to expand the hierarchy of the organization to be able to search a user through it. We can use **Path()** DAX function for that. Below is a calculated column added to the Organization table;

Path = PATH(

  Organization[ID],

Organization[Manager ID]

)

Path function accepts two parameters; The ID column (ID column in the Organization table) and the parent ID column (Manager ID). as a result, we will have a string of values separated by "|" showing the entire hierarchy for that member of the organization.

Looking for the User Organization ID in the Hierarchy of Organization

Now that we know what are the organization IDs associated with the user, and also the hierarchy of the organization, we have to search in every row to find out and see if they match somewhere.

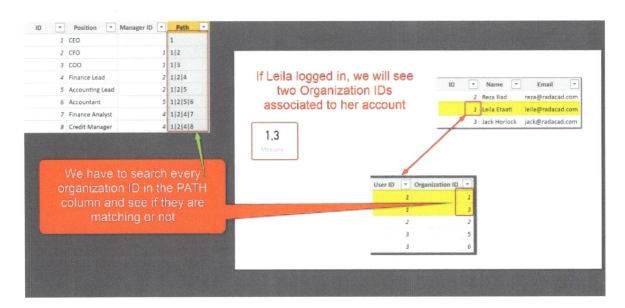

Implementing the Loop

Because the whole process should be dynamic based on the logged-in user, we cannot do that as a calculated column in the Organization table; we should do that in our measure calculation (continuing calculation from the previous chapter);

Measure =

CROSSJOIN(

  FILTER(

    'Users Organizations',

    'Users Organizations'[User ID]=

LOOKUPVALUE(

Users[ID],

Users[Email],

USERPRINCIPALNAME()

)

),

Organization)

As you can see, I removed the ConcatenateX because it was just for showing a view of the data in the table and did the **CrossJoin()** of the two tables. CrossJoin gets the name of tables and creates a cartesian product of rows in both tables. For each row in the Organization table, we will have all rows coming from the result of the Filter function (which is organizations associated with the current user).

I just put the expression above inside another ConcatenateX to show the values in there:

```
1  Measure =
2  CONCATENATEX(
3  CROSSJOIN(
4      FILTER(
5              'Users Organizations',
6              'Users Organizations'[User ID]=
7                  LOOKUPVALUE(
8                      Users[ID],
9                      Users[Email],
10                     USERPRINCIPALNAME()
11                 )
12          ),
13      Organization),
14      Organization[ID]&"-"&'Users Organizations'[Organization ID],
15      ",")
```

1-1,1-3,2-1,2-3,3-1,3-3,4-1,4-3,5-1,5-3,6-1,6-3,7-1,7-3,8-1,8-3

Measure

Checking if the Path contains the current user's organization ID

Now that we have created the loop structure using CrossJoin function, we can add a column to that virtual table and see if the path column in each row contains the current user's organization ID or not, we can do that using **AddColumn()** function in DAX;

Measure =

ADDCOLUMNS(

  CROSSJOIN(

   FILTER(

     'Users Organizations',

     'Users Organizations'[User ID]=

      LOOKUPVALUE(

       Users[ID],

       Users[Email],

       USERPRINCIPALNAME()

)

    ),

   Organization),

  "Path Contains This Organization",

  PATHCONTAINS(

   Organization[Path],

   [Organization ID])

)

AddColumns will add a column to the existing table, using three parameters; The table to add the column to it (The output table from CrossJoin step), Name of the New Column ("Path Contains This Organization"), and the expression for this column (PathContains). **PathContains()** is a DAX function that checks if a path does contain a value in it or not. I have written about Path and parent-child functions in a separate article, which I encourage you to read here.

The output of the expression above is still a table and cannot be visualized. However, if you use another ConcatenateX to see the output table, this is how it looks like;

Measure =

CONCATENATEX(

ADDCOLUMNS(

  CROSSJOIN(

   FILTER(

     'Users Organizations',

     'Users Organizations'[User ID]=

      LOOKUPVALUE(

       Users[ID],

       Users[Email],

       USERPRINCIPALNAME()

)

    ),

   Organization),

  "Path Contains This Organization",

  PATHCONTAINS(

  Organization[Path],

  [Organization ID])

),

Organization[Path]&"-"&'Users Organizations'[Organization ID]&"-"&[Path Contains This Organization],

  "

")

The output of the above expression looks like below;

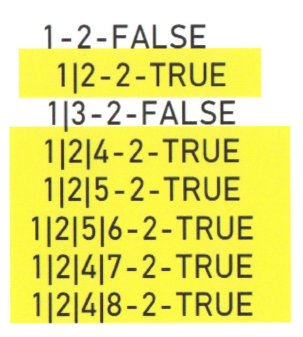

All of the rows that show TRUE are the rows that this user is somewhere in the organization path of it, so as a result, we have to only filter these rows.

Filtering only rows that this user is part of the organization hierarchy of those

Finally, let's filter only rows with True in their calculated column, which we filtered above. we can do that easily with a **FILTER()** function;

Measure =

FILTER(

  ADDCOLUMNS(

   CROSSJOIN(

    FILTER(

     'Users Organizations',

     'Users Organizations'[User ID]=

      LOOKUPVALUE(

Users[ID],

Users[Email],

USERPRINCIPALNAME()

)

),

Organization),

"Path Contains This Organization",

PATHCONTAINS(

Organization[Path],

[Organization ID])

),

[Path Contains This Organization])

The output would be similar to this (I used ConcatenateX for it);

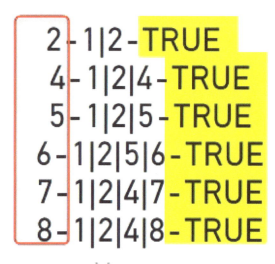

Measure

Now from the output above, we want to fetch a distinct list of Organization[ID] columns, and let's say the distinct output of that.

A distinct list of Organization IDs

As the last step of this DAX expression, I am using **SelectColumns()** to only select the Organization ID column from the table output from the previous step, and then getting a **Distinct()** output of that;

```
Measure =

DISTINCT(

  SELECTCOLUMNS(

    FILTER(

      ADDCOLUMNS(

        CROSSJOIN(

          FILTER(

            'Users Organizations',

            'Users Organizations'[User ID]=

              LOOKUPVALUE(

                Users[ID],

                Users[Email],

                USERPRINCIPALNAME()

              )

          ),

          Organization),

        "Path Contains This Organization",

        PATHCONTAINS(

          Organization[Path],
```

```
            [Organization ID])

        ),

        [Path Contains This Organization]),

      "Organization ID",

      Organization[ID]

  )

)
```

The output of the expression above (using ConcatenateX) looks like this:

2,4,5,6,7,8

Measure

Set the Role

Now, the hard part is done! we are ready to set the role. All we need to do is to filter the Organization Table that the Organization ID column in that table is in one of the values output from the expression above. I start this with going to Manage Roles under the Modeling Section;

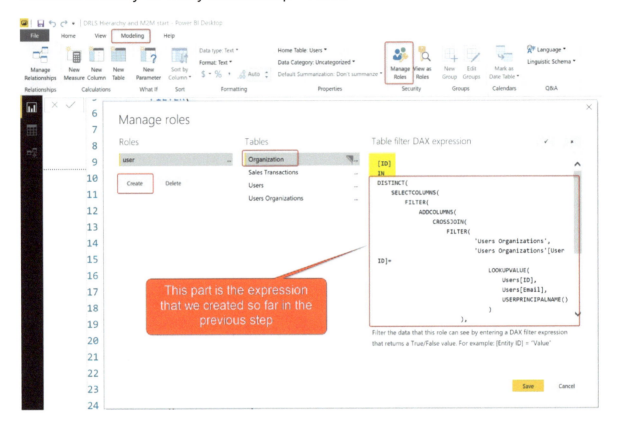

The whole row-level-security expression is here:

[ID]

IN

DISTINCT(

  SELECTCOLUMNS(

    FILTER(

      ADDCOLUMNS(

      CROSSJOIN(

      FILTER(

        'Users Organizations',

        'Users Organizations'[User ID]=

        LOOKUPVALUE(

```
                Users[ID],

                Users[Email],

                USERPRINCIPALNAME()

            )

        ),

    Organization),

"Path Contains This Organization",

PATHCONTAINS(

    Organization[Path],

    [Organization ID])

    ),

    [Path Contains This Organization]),

"Organization ID",

Organization[ID]

)

)
```

Testing the solution

Now, let's test the solution and see the output. As you can see below; I have added a few other measures to show the current user's name, and also current positions;

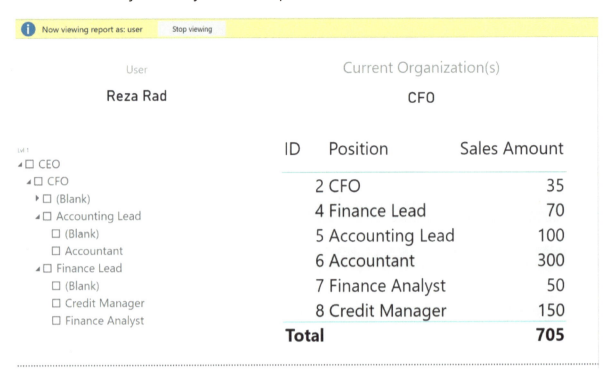

As you can see in the above view, Reza is CFO and will see everything except information about the CEO and COO.

Now, if I make Reza a CEO (that is how easy it is to become a CEO in our organization ;), and also COO, he will see everything;

User			
Reza Rad			

Current Organization(s)

CEO, COO

ID	Position	Sales Amount
2	CFO	35
3	COO	340
4	Finance Lead	70
5	Accounting Lead	100
6	Accountant	300
7	Finance Analyst	50
Total		**1065**

Lvl 1
- CEO
  - (Blank)
  - CFO
    - (Blank)
    - Accounting Lead
      - (Blank)
      - Accountant
    - Finance Lead
      - (Blank)
      - Credit Manager
      - Finance Analyst
- COO

Dynamic Row-level Security in Power BI with Organizational Hierarchy and Multiple Positions in Many-to-Many Relationship – Part 2

Because of the row-level-security defined on the Organization table, the User table, and User Organization table won't be filtered when the user logs in, You can hide the User Organization table, and then use a measure like this for the current user:

Current User = LOOKUPVALUE(

Users[Name],

Users[Email],

USERPRINCIPALNAME())

and a measure like this for all the current positions:

Current Organization =

CONCATENATEX(

FILTER(

Organization,

Organization[ID] in

SELECTCOLUMNS(

FILTER(

'Users Organizations',

'Users Organizations'[User ID]=

LOOKUPVALUE(

Users[ID],

Users[Email],

USERPRINCIPALNAME()

)

),

"Organization ID",

81

'Users Organizations'[Organization ID])

)

,Organization[Position],", ")

These two measures are used in the below report as you can see;

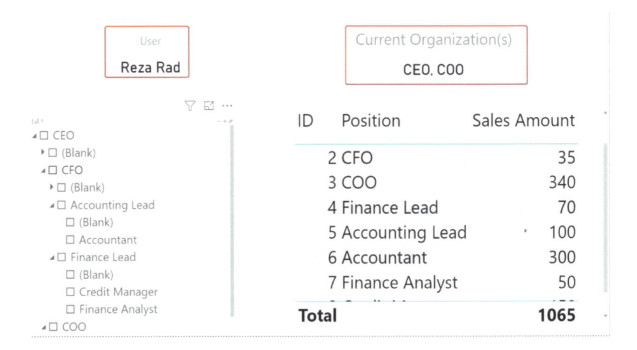

Summary

Implementing row-level-security can be challenging in scenarios such as what you
have seen in this chapter. You have seen a combination of organizational hierarchy,
and the many-to-many relationship brings some challenges in the implementation.
However, using DAX, you can solve all the challenges. The expression I mentioned
here used some functions such as Filter, SelectColumns, Distinct, CrossJoin,
LookupValue, AddColumns and etc. There are many other methods of writing the
rule in DAX.

Calculating Total, and Percentages in a Row-Level Security Power BI Model

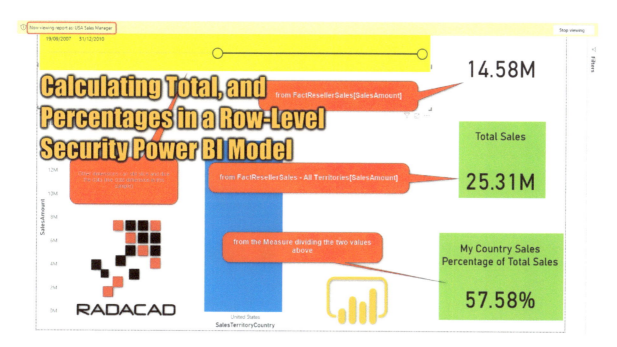

You have seen some samples about row-level security so far and learned different methods in which you can reduce the amount of data rows that a user can see based on their roles. However, in my presentations, I still get this question that: What if I want to compare the branch data against the total, but I don't want the user to see other branch's data. My approach to solving that is always an aggregated table. Let me walk you through a sample of it in this chapter.

Introduction

Row-Level Security in Power BI means limiting the access to the data rows in an existing Power BI dataset or report. Let's say; you share a Power BI report with user 1 and user 2, but you want them to see only part of the data from the whole report, not the entire data. You want user 1 to see, for example, sales of USA, and user 2 to see sales of Canada. This is something you can do with row-level security, and in earlier chapters of this book, I explained the basics of it.

For example, you can have a report which looks like below:

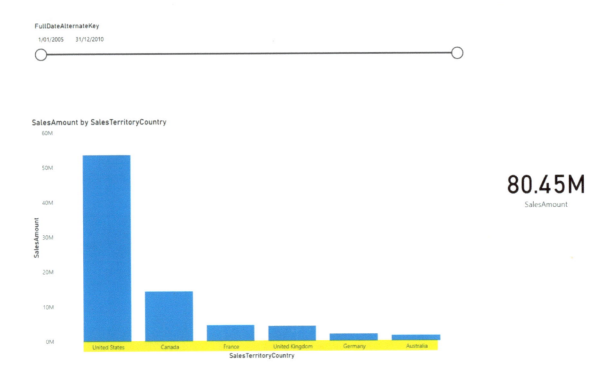

Which has information about all countries, and then you can apply row-level security that limits the access for some users, and they see only part of the data, like this:

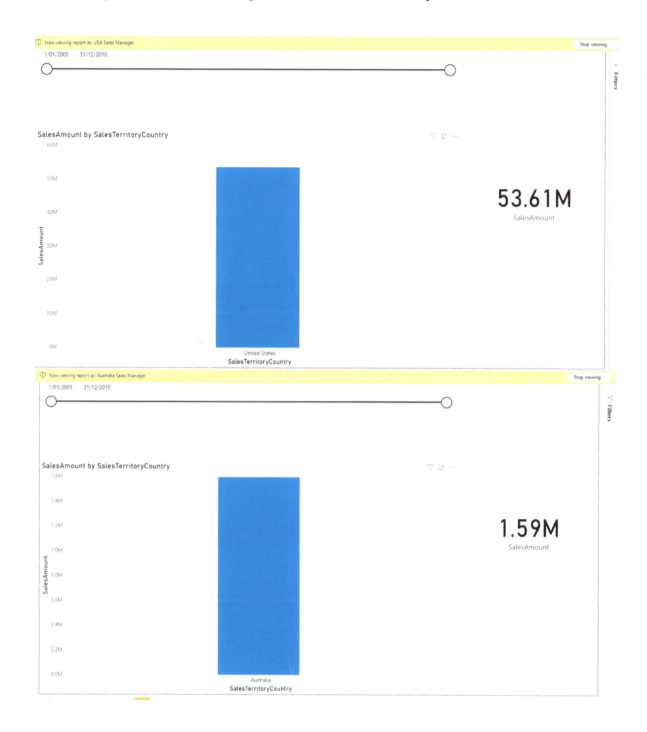

The Challenge

One of the challenges in the above implementation is that how you can access the total level data (average, sum) without exposing the details. Let's say that the sales manager of the United States wants to compare his sales with total sales and see how much percentage of the total sales across all countries belong to his region. Unfortunately, using DAX functions such as ALL or other functions that change the scope of the filter won't give you much luck. Because the row-level security is applied on the dataset table level before setting the filter context.

I usually do this with an aggregated table for the total values. Users don't need to learn about the details of other countries; they just need a total of all countries. so this can be an aggregated table with no country information in it. Let's see that through an example:

Sample Model

I am using the AdventureWorksDW2012 Excel dataset, which you can download here. and I am using these tables: DimSalesTerritory, DimDate, DimProduct, and FactResellerSales.

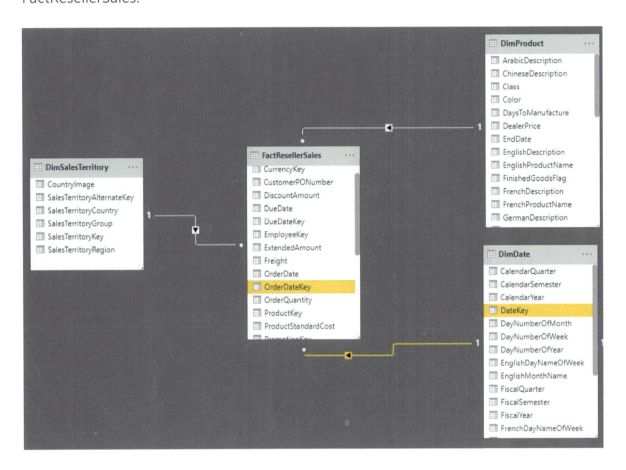

Create the Aggregated Table

You can create this aggregated table anywhere: in the data source using T-SQL or other database languages, or in Power Query using Group By or any other places you are more comfortable doing the aggregation. I use Power Query because that is the method you can use regardless of the data source.

The first step is to create a copy of FactResellerSales table, then Group By in the Power Query Editor;

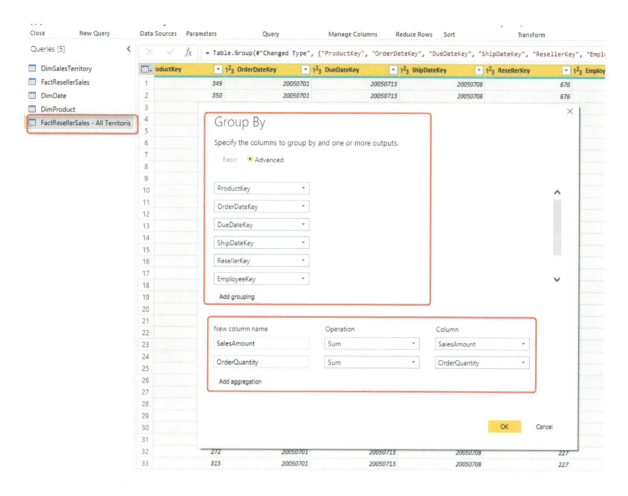

For this Group By operation, I use all key fields in the FactResellerSales except SalesTerritoryKey (because that is the field that connects this table to DimSalesTerritory, which is going to have the row-level security filter enabled on it). You can also add as many aggregations you want as Sum, Min, Max, Average, etc.

Add the Aggregated table to the model

In a very simple data model, your aggregated table might be only returning one row: the total. However, if your data model is slicing and dicing by multiple dimension tables, then it is likely that you need to connect your aggregated table to other tables. Our sample here is one of those too. I connect the aggregated table to the DimProduct and DimDate, but not to the DimSalesTerrirory because now this aggregated table has the totals of all territories.

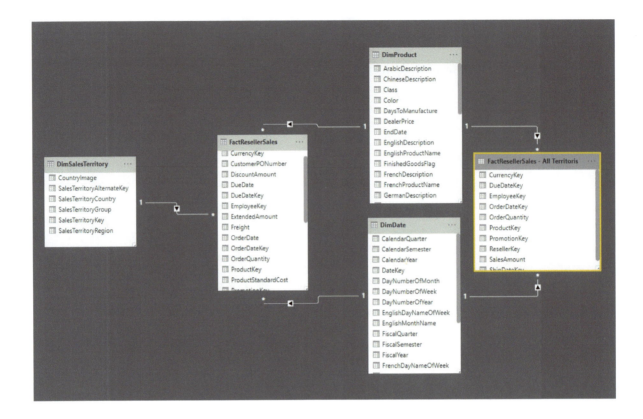

Row-Level Security Definition

In this sample example, I have used static row-level security. However, the same approach with slight changes can be used for dynamic row-level security too. here are my roles:

Testing the Solution

Well, that's pretty much all of it in terms of the modeling. To test the work, you can create a measure such as below:

My Country Sales vs Total Sales = SUM(FactResellerSales[SalesAmount])/SUM('FactResellerSales - All

Territoris'[SalesAmount])

and show it on a page with other visuals:

Now, if you try to view this as a user, let's say United States Sales Manager user, this is what you see:

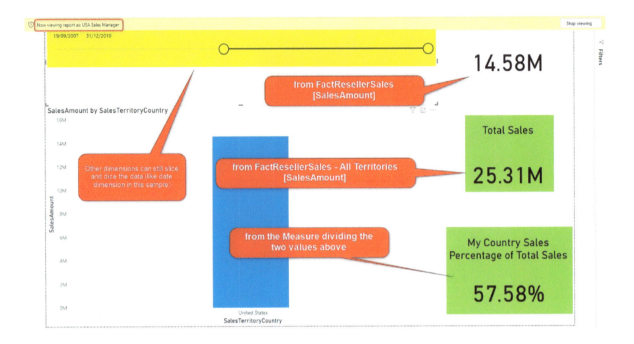

You can see that the detailed table (FactInternetSales) got filtered by the row-level security configuration. However, the total table only gets filtered by other dimensions (such as date table in this case), not the DimSalesTerritory.

How to Implement it with Dynamic Row-Level Security?

If you are implementing this in a dynamic row-level security approach, then the aggregated table should not be connected to your user table (in simple DRLS scenarios). However, for more complex scenarios, you need to think about how to implement it. for example, you might want other users to see the total of higher-level organizational hierarchy or something, which depends on that the aggregated table should be created and connected to the model.

Summary

In Summary, this chapter was an explanation of the aggregated table approach used to enhance the row-level security based dataset, so that you can calculate values vs. total, or percentages or etc.

Row-level Security with SSAS Tabular Live Connection in Power BI

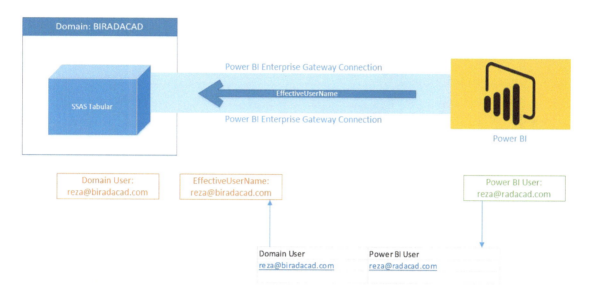

You can define Row-level Security in Power BI itself. However sometimes you do use SQL Server Analysis Services Tabular as the source for Power BI through Live or DirectQuery connection. SSAS Tabular allows you to create the same type of Row-level Security. So it would be much better to use Row-level Security defined in Tabular from Power BI, rather than duplicating that in Power BI. In this chapter I'll show you an end-to-end solution which contains elements below;

- Power BI Live Connect to SSAS Tabular through Enterprise Gateway
- Row-level Security Configuration in SSAS Tabular
- Viewing the result filtered by RLS in Power BI

Note that this method is different from defining Row-level Security in Power BI Desktop. This is implementing the same approach but in SSAS.

Prerequisite

For this demo, I will be using my demo machine, which has SSAS Tabular and Enterprise Gateway. You also need to have SSAS Tabular database example AW Internet Sales Tabular Model 2014 from here.

Install and Configure Enterprise Gateway

The purpose of gateways in Power BI is to create the connection from Power BI cloud service to on-premises data sources. There are two types of gateways; Enterprise, and Personal. The naming of these gateways is a bit misleading. Personal doesn't mean you have to install the gateway on your laptop only, and Enterprise doesn't mean only for organizations. There are more differences as well, which I skip here for simplicity. In general, Enterprise is built for more live connections specially to Analysis Services, and Personal is more for importing data from many data sources. Let's leave details of that for now. For this example, we will be using Enterprise Gateway because we want to connect to SSAS Tabular on-premises through a Live/DirectQuery connection.

You can download the latest version of Enterprise Gateway from PowerBI.Microsoft.Com website under downloads

Then from the gateways download page, choose Enterprise gateway, and download it.

Installation of Enterprise Gateway is just following a wizard, so continue that till the end of the wizard where it asks for Power BI login. Sign in to your Power BI account;

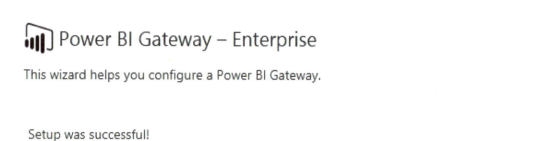

This wizard helps you configure a Power BI Gateway.

Setup was successful!

To configure the gateway, you must first sign in to Power BI.

Sign in to Power BI   Cancel

After sign in, configure the Power BI Gateway with a name and key, and then you should be good to go. If you see a green checkbox and Connected means your configuration was successful.

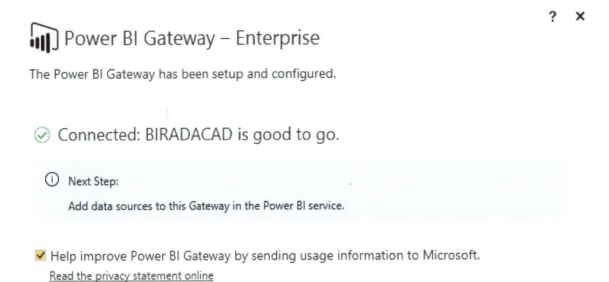

As you can see after a successful configuration, you can close the gateway (don't worry it is running behind the scene as a service), and add a data source to this gateway in Power BI Service.

Or alternatively, you can directly go to Power BI website, after login go to setting menu option and choose Manage Gateways

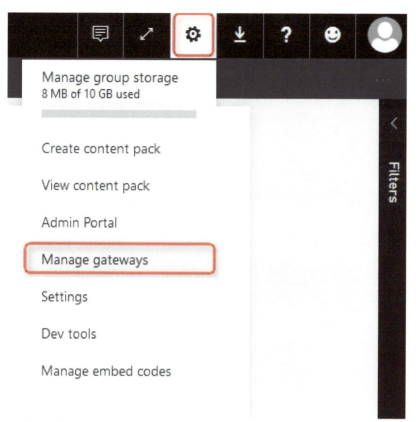

In the Gateway management window, you can see all the gateways you have set up. My gateway here is named BIRADACAD, and I can see that it is successfully connected.

Gateways

+ADD DATA SOURCE

> RezaSurface ⚠

> BIRADACAD

Test all connections

Gateway Settings   Administrators

✓ Online: You are good to go.

Gateway Name

BIRADACAD

Department

Description

Contact Information

Reza@⬛⬛⬛⬛⬛⬛⬛⬛⬛.com

Apply   Discard

Create Data Source

Now Let's create Data Sources. You might think that one gateway is enough for connecting to all data sources in a domain. That is absolutely right. However, you still need to add a data source under that gateway per each source. each source can be a SQL Server database, Analysis Services database and etc. For this example, we are building a data source for SQL Server Analysis Tabular on-premises. Before going through this step; I have installed AW Internet Sales Tabular Model 2014 on my SSAS Tabular, and want to connect to it. If you don't have this database, follow the instruction in the prerequisite section.

For creating a data source, click on Add Data Source in manage gateways window (you have to select the right gateway first)

Gateways

+ADD DATA SOURCE

> RezaSurface ⚠

> BIRADACAD

Test all connections

Then enter details for the data source. I named this data source as AW Internet Sales Tabular Model 2014, I enter my server name, and database name. then I use Windows authentication with my domain user <domain>\username and the password. You should see a successful message after clicking on Apply. The domain name that I use is BIRADACAD (my SSAS Tabular domain), and the user is PBIgateway, which is a user of the BIRADACAD domain (username: BIRADACAD\PBIgateway) and is an administrator for SSAS Tabular (explained in next few paragraphs).

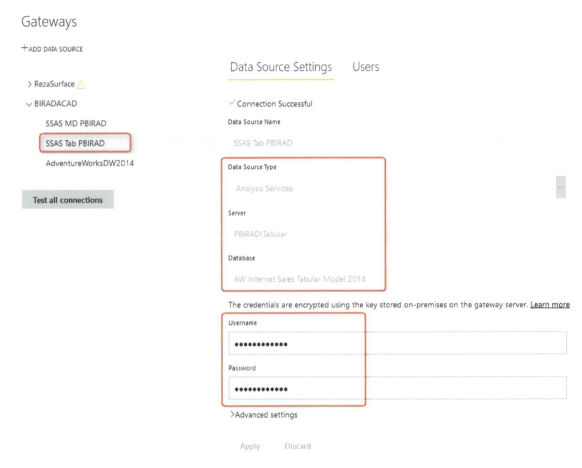

Note that the user account that you are using here should meet these conditions:

- It should be a Domain User
- The domain user should be an administrator in SSAS Tabular.

You can set administrator for SSAS Tabular with right-clicking on SSAS Tabular instance in SSMS and in Properties window,

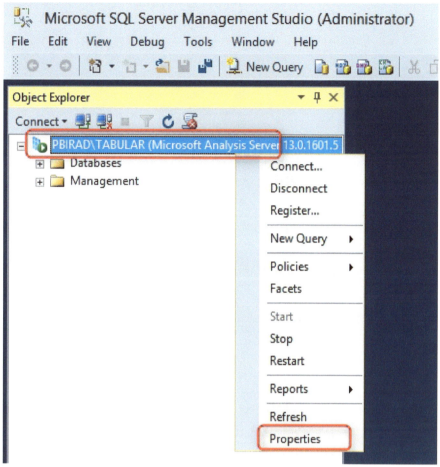

in the Security setting, add the user to the administrators' list.

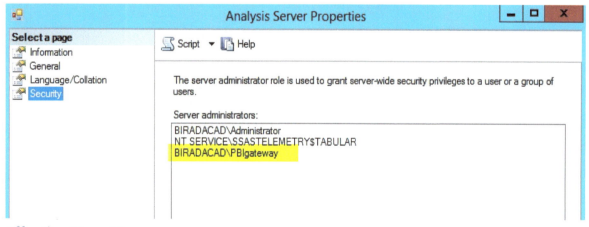

Effective User Name

Gateway account used for accessing Power BI cloud service to on-premises SSAS Tabular. However, this account by itself isn't enough for the data retrieval. the gateway then passes the EffectiveUserName from Power BI to on-premises SSAS Tabular, and the result of the query will be returned based on the access of the EffectiveUserName account to the SSAS Tabular database and model.

By default, EffectiveUserName is the username of logged in user to Power BI, or in other words, EffectiveUserName is the Power BI account. This means your Power BI account should have enough access to SSAS Tabular database to fetch the required data. If the Power BI account is the account from the same domain as SSAS Tabular, then there is no problem, and security configuration can be set in SSAS Tabular (explained later in this chapter). However, if domains are different, then you have to do UPN mapping.

UPN Mapping

Your SSAS Tabular is part of a domain (it should be actually because that's how Live connection works), and that domain might be the domain that your Power BI user account is. If you are using the same domain user for the Power BI account, then you can skip this step. If you have a separate Power BI user account than the domain account for SSAS Tabular, then you have to set the UPN Mapping.

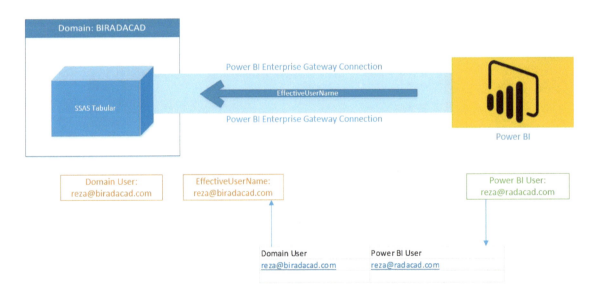

UPN Mapping, in simple definition, will map Power BI accounts to your local on-premises SSAS Tabular domain accounts. Because in my example, I don't use the same domain account for my Power BI account, so I set up UPN as below.

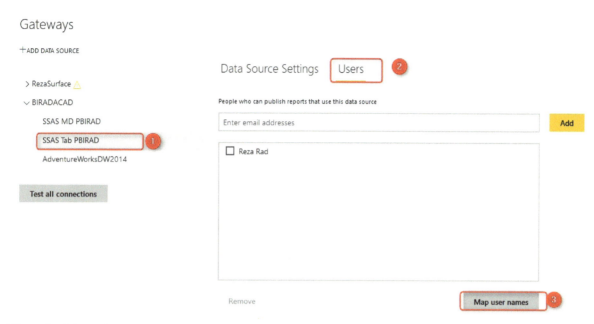

Then in Mapping pane, I create a new mapping that maps my Power BI user account to reza@biradacad.com, which is my local domain for SSAS Tabular server.

Map user names

Create rules to map user names to Analysis Services server user names or associate custom data with user names. Learn more

Select the type of rule for this data source

○ Effective user names   1
○ CustomData

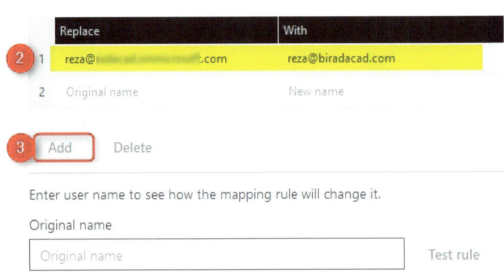

Replace	With
1 reza@••••••••••.com	reza@biradacad.com
2 Original name	New name

3   **Add**   Delete

Enter user name to see how the mapping rule will change it.

Original name

Original name	Test rule

After rule applied

Result of applying mapping rule will appear here

OK   Cancel

Now with this user name mapping, reza@biradacad.com will be passed as EffectiveUserName to the SSAS Tabular. If you want to learn more about UPN mapping, you can watch Adam Saxton's great video about it.

Configure Row-level Security in SSAS Tabular

In SSAS Tabular opened in SSMS, expand AW Internet Sales Tabular Model 2014, and create a New Role

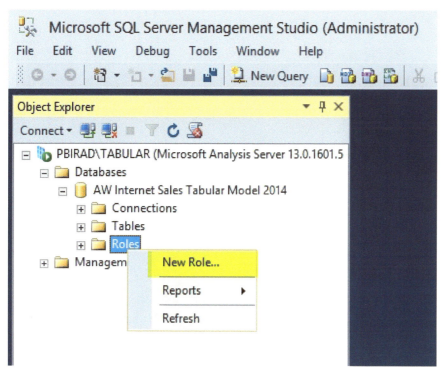

We want to create a role for users who don't have access to Bike sales across the database. so let's name the role as No Bike Sales Manager, this role has Read access to the database.

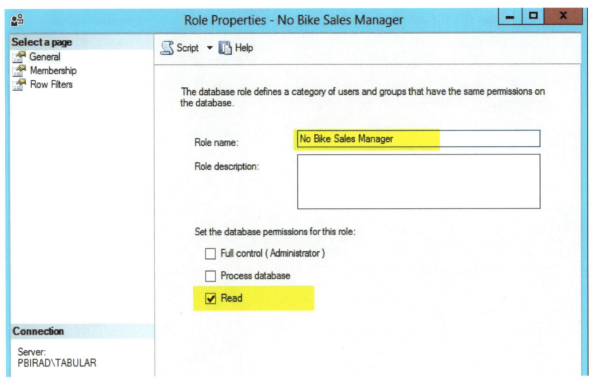

In the membership section, you can add users to this role. Users should be domain users that you get through EffectiveUserName from Power BI (if Power BI accounts aren't domain users, then create UPN mapping for them as explained above in the UPN mapping section). I add user BIRADACAD\Reza here. (Note that I've created a UPN mapping for this user. so each time Power BI user associated with this logs in, this domain account will be passed through EffectiveUserName to SSAS Tabular).

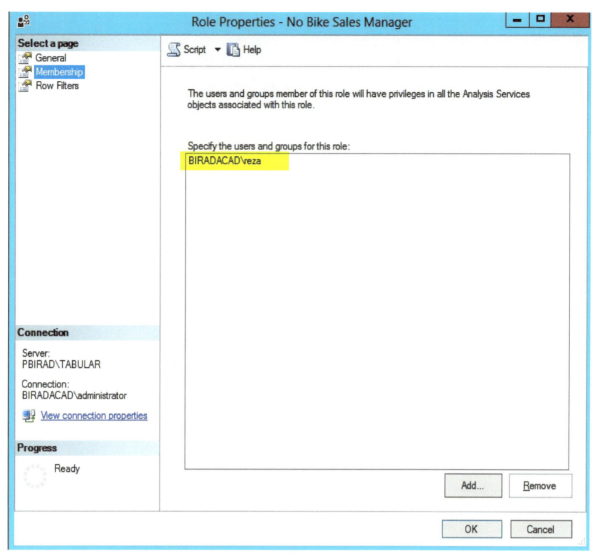

Now let's define Row Filters with a basic filter on Product Category as below;

='Product Category'[Product Category Name]<>'Bikes'

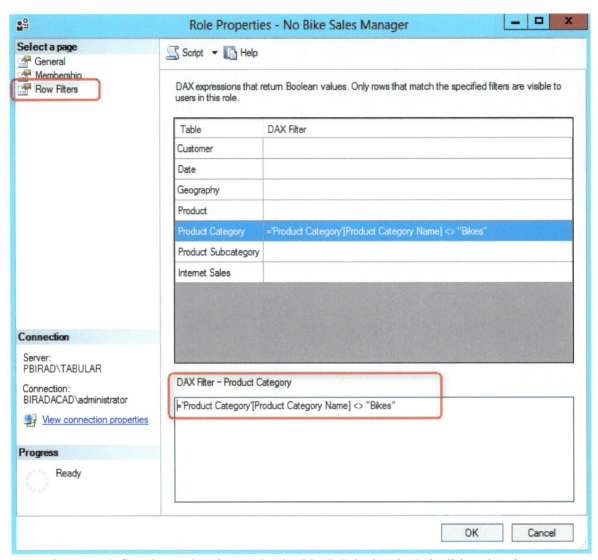

Now that we defined row-level security in SSAS Tabular, let's build a simple report to test it.

Create a Sample Report

Our sample report here would only show a Pie chart of Product Categories Sales. To create a Live connection to SSAS Tabular from Power BI Desktop.

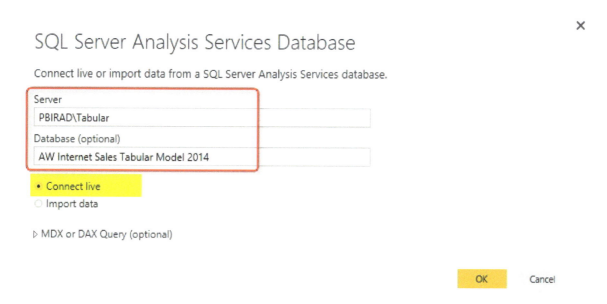

Then choose the model

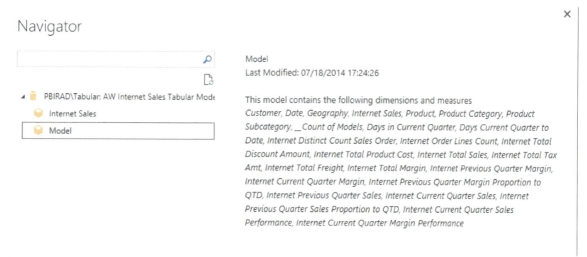

After creating the connection, you should see the Live Connection: Connected status in Power BI Desktop down right-hand side corner.

Create a simple Pie chart with Product Category Name (from Product Category table) as Legend and Sales Amount (from Internet Sales table) as Values.

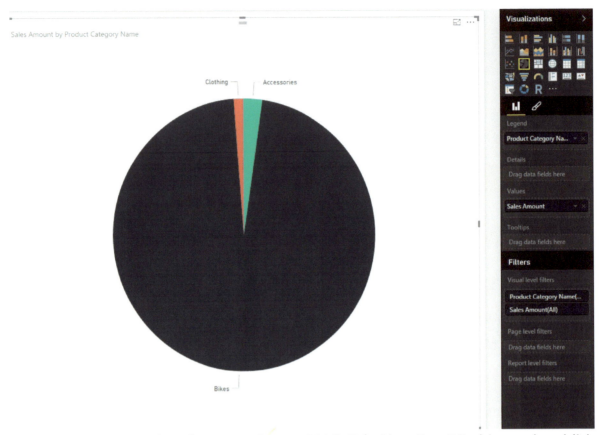

Save the Power BI file, for example, as SSAS Tab Live Ent DB.pbix, and publish it. **Remember that you shouldn't set up Row-level Security in Power BI itself**. Because we will be using RLS configuration from Live Tabular connection.

Test the Result

In Power BI website or service, when you login, and refresh the SSAS Tab Live Ent DB report. you won't see any sales from Bikes. you will only see sales of Clothing and Accessories.

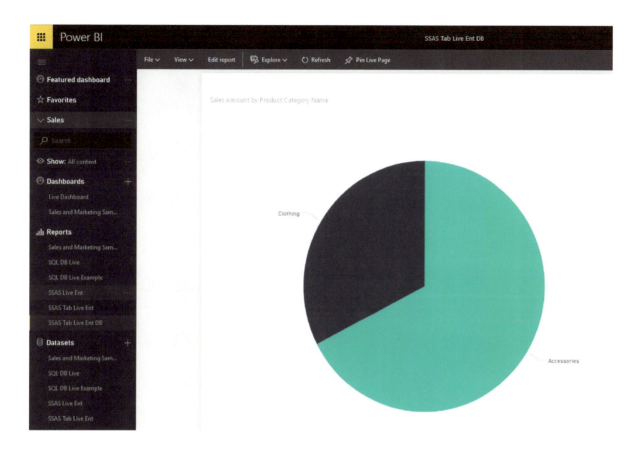

How doesn't it work?

What happened here is that my Power BI account mapped to reza@biradacad.com domain user, and this domain user passed through enterprise gateway as the EffectiveUserName to the SSAS Tabular on-premises. SSAS Tabular identified that this user has only one role, which is No Bike Sales Manager, and this role has a restricted view of sales for everything but Bike. So the data returned from SSAS Tabular to Power BI report doesn't contain Bike's sales.

Summary

SSAS Tabular as a Live connection source for Power BI used in many enterprise solutions for Power BI. There are different reasons for that, for example;

- Some organizations already have SSAS Tabular models ready, and they are using that for their on-premises reporting and data analysis. So they want to use the same source of truth.
- The scale of data is larger than it fits into the Power BI model. (Read step beyond 10GB limitation for Power BI as an example).
- and many other reasons.

In this chapter, you've seen how Row-level Security defined in SSAS Tabular will be passed through EffectiveUserName to Power BI accounts. This method will authorize users to only view part of the data that they are authorized to see.